No Tears for Twenty Years

No Tears for Twenty Years

CLIVE GUEST

StoryTerrace

Text Clive Guest
Copyright © Clive Guest and StoryTerrace
Text is private and confidential

First print January 2025

www.StoryTerrace.com

CONTENTS

1: FROM LITTLE 'UN TO A LIFE LIVED LARGE — 9

2: EARLY YEARS ALONG COMMON ROAD — 21

3: SNICK AND THE GREAT OUTDOORS — 37

4: THE DAY EVERYTHING CHANGED — 51

5: ROARING THROUGH MY TEENAGE YEARS — 73

6: SETTLING DOWN TO MANAGERIAL LIFE — 91

7: A DOUBLE WEDDING IS ANNOUNCED! — 97

8: NOW I UNDERSTAND … — 107

9: PROMOTION AND PROMOTIONS! — 115

10: ONE IN A MILLION – TIMES FOUR! — 141

11: ADVENTURES IN AFRICA — 171

12: WHEN ONE DOOR CLOSES ...   **185**

13: ALCOHOL AND OTHER ADDICTIONS: THEIR ROLE IN MY STORY   **195**

14: RETURNING TO THE SHOP FLOOR   **203**

15: STILL SO MUCH AHEAD   **209**

GLOSSARY: NICKNAMES AND THEIR ORIGINS   **217**

1: FROM LITTLE 'UN TO A LIFE LIVED LARGE

'**G**reat news, Gladys – it's a girl!'

With two small but lively boys already, I can only imagine how happy Mom must have been to hear this called out confidently to her by the midwife, Nurse Roberts, one seasonably sultry August day in 1942. By coincidence, Nurse Roberts lived in the next house but one. Exhausted from labouring at home in the upstairs front bedroom of 18 Common Road, Wombourne, South Staffordshire, Mom was now awaiting the moment she would hold her newborn in her arms.

'We'll call her Olive,' Mom said to her friend and next-door neighbour Nell, who'd been at the birth and was now on hand with encouragement and fresh, clean towels. 'Olive Guest.'

It was 23rd August 1942, at around 11 a.m. Gladys's husband, Ben, wasn't away fighting in the Second World War. I am not entirely sure why, because his job as an enameller at a factory wasn't classified as essential work. Dad wasn't at the birth because this wasn't 'the done thing' in the 1940s. I rather think he was at work. He used to go there on his motorbike. At other times, he was out on Home Guard duties. He had joined the Home Guard as a volunteer to patrol the streets and help get everyone into shelters when air raids were expected. In fact, there was even an air-raid shelter in our garden, so when there were air raids, Dad had the peace of mind that we didn't have to travel that far to be safe. There was, thankfully, no air raid on this day and all was peace and calm, that's to say as much as it ever can be when a baby is born.

'Wait!' said Nurse Roberts, just before Nell headed for the stairs, ready to dash onto the street and spread the news. 'I am sorry, Gladys – it's another boy.'

'Ben will be pleased,' said Nell, reaching for her friend's hand. 'He's such a great dad to your boys.'

A new name was swiftly selected. Arthur was the name of Mom's brother, change the 'O' for a 'C' and Olive would become Clive.

Arthur Clive Guest. But always Clive.

By that teatime, *my* unceremonious arrival into the world would have been celebrated by all the families that knew ours in what was a very tight-knit community, and at Wombourne Ferro Enamels, where my dad, Ben, was working.

My brothers, Larry, then four, and Irwin, two, were also delighted. And in a way, it didn't matter too much what my hastily thought up first name was, because whilst I dropped the Arthur to be called Clive at school and ever since, Mom and most of her friends always knew us three boys as Big 'Un, Middle 'Un and Little 'Un! My Uncle Arthur called me 'Murphy' – no real reason other than it was the name of a potato that was especially popular when he served with the Irish Fusiliers. Then, the mum of my best boyhood mate, Terry Stone – always called Snick – gave me the nickname Bab-Babs, which also stuck. Even today in our 80s, he calls me Bab-Babs and I call him Snick!

In the 1940s, everybody in Wombourne had a nickname – or three. Sometimes, the reasons for these names were obvious – Mom's names for her sons, in age order, for example. At other times, there was a story attached. So Snick's mum was always called Dirty Legs. I'll come onto that story presently in the Glossary, as well as many more anecdotes and recollections that it's been my pleasure to put into chronological order.

So why am I writing this book? Well, first off, it has to be because I can. I count it a blessing that I have a brilliant memory for names, places, events and for an extraordinary level of detail, right back to recalling being a babe in arms when, at Auntie Alma's wedding, I put my hand down Mom's top as I always did as a baby. I wonder if this had an influence on my always being a breast man! I can remember scenes from my life in full, and that's been a true gift: from the summer when Snick and I wreaked havoc by blowing up a tree with bombs we'd painstakingly created from batteries and iron fillings, to the exact phrases customers said to me at my first retail job in Pearks, Wolverhampton, in 1957. I have total recall, which is just what you need when you are writing your life story.

Pearks grocery chain had the slogan 'The store that never sells a bad egg', and everything was counter service. I learnt how to bone a side of bacon – courtesy of Elsie Ramsbottom, whom I cheekily nicknamed Sheep's Arse, but never said so in her hearing! – plus how to skin enormous, 80-pound blocks of Cheddar cheese and to always keep calm and polite. When I began my first job, I was only 4 feet 8 inches tall and had to stand on an empty cheese box to reach the bacon slicer. There were no rigorous health and safety rules then, although today it is only a tick-box exercise. But there were perks of being at Pearks, such as working alongside lots of girls in the store!

Such is my memory, I can recall a good many of my encounters with both staff and customers. For example, I remember a customer saying to me, 'How much are your large eggs, son?'

I replied, 'Four pennies each, Sir.' (In those days, everyone was Sir or Madam.)

'How much are the cracked ones?'

'Two pennies, Sir.'

'Then crack me a dozen large!'

I took to the work at once and was encouraged by my manager, who said to me after a couple of weeks, 'If you get on well here, son, you will never be out of a job, because people have always got to eat.'

Wise words that I heeded over a lifetime, which leads me to the second reason why I have written this book: I have worked with hundreds of great colleagues. I went on to enjoy a brilliant 40-year career managing ever-bigger supermarket stores. Whenever we get together, as we did this very summer at a celebration football event between Evesham Tesco and

Argyll United (my old team), the subject of 'old times' comes up. Their response is always the same. 'Clive, you must write a book about it . . .'

So yes, be assured – the hard work and success, plus the larger-than-life characters and the perks of managing a store in the 1970s and 1980s that meant I never had to pay for the likes of cigarettes, alcohol or kids' bikes – it's all here. Life in retail in the 1960s, 1970s and 1980s was different from today. I worked smart and hard. My staff loved how I treated them. All the stores I managed were profitable.

Reason number three for writing this book, however, is the one that made me determined to stop thinking and start writing. I wanted to share the full story of my life with my sons, Carl and Steven, and their children. At my age, you never know when JC will call you upstairs. I don't want the many good times I have enjoyed and the life lessons learnt from them to be lost.

Boys – I know we have a great relationship, and over the years, we have talked for hour after hour. Yet there is so much more I want you to know. Growing up in the 1940s and early 1950s, I led an outdoor childhood in a world so different from the one you arrived into. Can you imagine the freedom that comes with being just seven or so years old and leaving the house at breakfast with just the one instruction to be home before it gets dark? Or the restriction and quiet fear that come with knowing that if you speak out of turn, at school or home, you are liable for a clip around the ear – or worse – from a teacher or Mom? An exception to this was my dad. He never laid a finger on any of us children, and I never heard him swear. Would you believe I never even heard him say the word 'bloody'.

In general, though, my generation had to get on with whatever life threw their way. I've never been more than even a single week out of work, which still stands today as I continue to put in a 37-hour week at Morrisons, Stratford-upon-Avon, even at 81 years old! And the best of it is I still enjoy retail.

For more than 20 years, Beryl, my children and I have owned a house in Gambia, where we used to spend the winter months. You'll read later about the quirk of fate that led to our discovering this beautiful part of Africa. I began writing this book in Gambia, in longhand and using a school exercise book. Snatching moments at 6 a.m., and before anyone else was up, I'd sit outside before the day's heat had begun and jot down key dates, names and places. From starting work three days after my 15th birthday to managing my first store from the age of just 17 to bringing in a cool million pounds of profit for Presto and then Safeway, time after time, my notes grew and grew. I ensured that I included the truly significant events too – which, of course, means family, and in particular, the arrivals of my much-loved grandchildren: Carl's two, Adam and Lauren, and Steve's daughter, Cynthia, now aged 27, 23 and 17 respectively.

Whilst colleagues said I should write the book, it was family who wanted to know why I'd chosen the title *No Tears for 20 Years*.

I declined to reveal.

Even Beryl – my wife of more than 50 years – may find the answer a surprise when she gets to the chapter titled *Now I Understand*. It's a moment of my life I've never talked about.

On balance, I consider myself the luckiest of men. My ethos on life is that you get out what you put in. There have been personal challenges and times when it has felt that I have been up to my neck in water, including when a 19-foot flood meant we had to be rescued from the upstairs bedroom! But I have enjoyed good health and have had an extraordinary and contented life.

For sure, it has been one that could never have been predicted from my very humble beginnings. When I left school the month before my 15th birthday, the plan was that I would work in the Wolverhampton die-casting factory alongside Mom. It was noisy, smelly and overcrowded, but factory work was what working-class boys mostly did, or else they worked as gardeners or handymen on large landowners' estates, as my Uncle Arthur did. I hadn't passed any exams, but I hadn't *failed* any, either: like the rest of my class, the focus had been on basic maths, reading, writing and sport. We did not sit exams.

'I can't take you yet, lad,' the factory foreman explained. 'You'll need a National Insurance card that gets issued on your 15th birthday. Come back then.'

No way was I going to work in that noisy, dirty factory.

The following Friday, I went with Mom to the job centre in Wolverhampton.

'Have you thought about shop work?' said a lady behind the desk, handing me a vacancy card for Pearks.

'Not really,' I told her. But I went along to the Pearks store on Queen Street. The manager, Mr Tustin, showed me around and said I could start on Monday for £2 19 *s.* a week. About a month later, I was asked if I wanted to sign for an apprenticeship. This was a three-year programme, but, incredibly, it turned out that I got my own store to manage a year before that apprenticeship finished.

All these years on, I like to think the same character attributes that meant I did well at Pearks still apply. I say what I mean, try to do others a good turn and don't let quarrels fester. Friends have told me I am like an 'open book' because there's no side to me. Life is too short! So now, friends, family – especially Beryl and my boys – I invite you to open this book and read the story of my life.

Putting it together was satisfying and brought back smiles *and* tears. I've tried not to hold anything back. Please enjoy the read!

Clive Guest
Warwickshire, summer 2023

The Wodehouse Farm, Wombourne, where in the late '40s and early '50s, I would churn butter for four hours all for 2/6.

Wodehouse, Wombourne, Karen, Sal, me (Manicuring Beryl's toenails) and Neil, Karen's brother, Irwin's kids. Open day.

Beryl, looking her beautiful best, with me in tow. Happy Days. Love you.

Lauren, Carl and Liza's, Daughter, at the Wodehouse, Wombourne. Another outing with Nanny Beryl.

a Lytch Gate, made out of farm implements, Wodehouse

2: EARLY YEARS ALONG COMMON ROAD

With farmlands belonging to Billy Lamb's family stretching into the distance on both sides and a winding brook that, in places, was now double the width thanks to a bomb from the Second World War exploding there, Common Road, Wombourne, was a great base for a young lad who liked being outdoors. Back in the 1940s, practically all mums sent their children packing (perhaps with a banana, certainly not with a full picnic and fizzy drinks!) and said that they could stay out from morning until dusk – and mine was no exception.

That was simply how families lived in those times. Children were not the centre of their parents' universe, as they are today.

Of course, when I was too small to be out on my own, I was mostly with Mom. An early memory is of her pushing me in my pram along Rookery Road then putting a young bird that was soaking wet into the front of the pram. This would have been after a downpour when, as today, this section of the road was covered in puddles. Very likely, Mom was pushing me to my grandma's, because she wanted to see her mother at the Wodehouse Estate. This grand country house and thousands of acres of land belonged to Miss Shaw-Hellier. Generations of Mom's family had worked there, as far back as my grandad's dad in the 19th century, and the family had a remote, tied cottage that went with their jobs. My grandad had been head gardener and Mom's never-married brother, Arthur, worked there and lived with them too. There will be more of him later in my story.

I can't remember Grandad on Mom's side, or my dad's side come to think of it. Both had passed on. But I do remember this grandma, who was called Sally. She was kind-hearted and would give me Quaker Oats porridge topped with treacle. When my friend Snick was with me, she would give him porridge, too. I remember a cracking day when we'd been watching my dad work on a civil defence building in Mill Lane and then, cold and hungry, we'd gone over to Grandma Sally's and she'd made sure we were warm and full of porridge. There was neither electricity nor running water in her cottage and cooking was done on the range fireplace. Due to her son's job in the gardens of the estate, there were always plenty of home-grown vegetables.

My gran's sister, and Uncle Jim, used to visit Grandma's cottage for two weeks' holiday in the summer with her daughter and grandaughter. She had moved to Ellesmere Port, Cheshire, and raised her family there. She was, I think, the only member of the family who had moved away from the village. Grandma Sally died at her own home. She was 73. I remember the 'death rattle' sound as she struggled to breathe during the last day or so of her life. I was holding Mom's hand, standing at the side of the bed, the same bed that I would be sleeping in when I was aged 16.

Mom had another brother, called Joe. He was visiting her one night when he was killed outside her cottage by one of the very few cars that were on the road in 1940s Britain. The car didn't stop and Joe was found in the road by Arthur. The driver, who lived 3 miles away at Sedgley, was found eventually and prosecuted. A big tragedy for our family.

Joe had a wife, May, and a daughter called Alma. For years after the accident, Alma would visit us at Common Road on Christmas mornings. I would be looking out for her (then in her early 20s) coming up the drive . . . I knew she would have with her a Rupert Bear Annual for me! It was my favourite present. I can't remember how old I was, but I recall sobbing one year as Alma arrived at Christmas without it. Obviously she thought I was getting too old for comic characters. Another much-liked Christmas present was the 'grab bag' that Dad and other workers at Ferro Enamels were given for their kids. It was full of small toys, plus an orange.

Mom also had another brother, called Jack, who was married to Annie and they lived in a village called Seisdon, not far from Wombourne. Jack would feature in my life for a reason I will come to later.

Whilst we saw Mom's family the most, Dad's family lived in Wombourne as well. I don't remember these grandparents or much about Dad's four brothers, either. One, called Fred, was nicknamed Tetnal, because he did all his courting under a pear tree, which was a Tetnal Dick variety.

Dad would be known as Wicket to his friends on account of his umpiring at the village cricket matches. I have many, many happy memories of watching Dad keep very good order on the cricket pitch. His friendly manner and strong sense of fair play made him the perfect umpire. As a small boy, I loved it when they stopped play for refreshments. These were served up by Lily Crowe, who ran the newsagent/corner shop/post office, and included the most delicious vanilla ice cream. This was freshly made by Lily's husband, Frank, and sold for 2 *d*. as a thick ice-cream slice inside two wafers or as a cornet. On non-match days, the Crowes sold ice cream in large jugs that you'd bring from home. More than seven decades on, I've never found anything to beat its rough texture and rich, creamy sweetness!

Lily was a huge woman and a real village character. Her shop had its own tea room to the back of the retail and post office area. It was in the centre of Wombourne, alongside a butcher, greengrocer and other essential shops, which included a barber, where a guy called Bert Bodison worked. When he cut my hair you would have thought he had put a basin on my head and cut around it. Nightmare! There was also a village green and tennis courts and a bowling green as well as the cricket pitch. These were situated opposite Lily Crowe's.

Running down the side of this road was a small gully with running spring water that we would race lollipop sticks in and also drink when it was a hot day.

Mom, my brothers and I also went with Dad when he umpired at away matches. We'd travel by Noakes coach and on the return people on the coach would sing songs. 'She'll be coming round the mountain' and 'If I knew you were coming, I would have baked you a cake' were the loudest!

Lots of people of my age say that it felt like summer used to be endless days of warmth and sunshine. I remember wearing a flat cap from the age of about four as most other young boys did in those days (it shielded us from the sun and it was copying what adult working-class men did, too), plus short trousers and the hot sun burning my legs. Certainly it's true that I can't remember many days in June, July or August that were blighted by rain or cold winds. It was a wonderful time to savour each year.

If summers were hot, winters were freezing! Indoors and out. We did have electricity for lighting, but with just the coal fire in the downstairs front room for heating, the bedroom I shared with my brothers was so cold that long shards of ice would form on the windowpane. You could pick them off to see how many moments you could bear to have them in your hands for as they melted.

Mom was big on keeping her kids clean. When I was small, she would sit me on the draining board and give me a wash in the kitchen sink!

During the war, so when I would have been no more than two or three years old, an evacuee called Billy Riley came to live in our house. Billy lived in Wolverhampton, which, due to its high number of factories, was a target for German bombers. Billy's father, John, ran a transport business and at one point my father had worked for him driving a lorry. John felt his son would be safer with us in the countryside.

There had been only one bomb explosion in Wombourne by the time Billy arrived. A German plane was hit by ack-ack guns and, just before it burst into flames and crashed, the crew dropped its bomb. As well as widening the brook, shrapnel from the bomb hit builder Bob Gouch's leg.

Bob, who lived around 200 yards from our house, had returned home from the air-raid shelter because his daughter, Tannis, was asleep inside in her pram and he didn't want to leave her for long. She was OK, and so Bob stood on the step, watching the flames from the struck plane. That was when he was hit.

He went on to have his leg amputated. Bob was a determined man who was somehow able to continue his work as a builder. By the late 1950s, Tannis was a stunner. Me and Snick would often see sports cars picking her up. Some years later, Bob's luck changed. He won £75,000 on Littlewoods Football Pools. That was when £75,000 was the maximum anyone could win.

The same didn't go for my dad's brother's son, Dennis Guest, who I recollect one Saturday placed an enormous bet on the football matches. It was so cold and wintry that a lot of the matches were called off and this was what his gamble was about. His bet was any eight draws from however many matches were played and he stipulated that he wouldn't place his bet if the pools panel met to decide the results of abandoned matches. But it backfired on Dennis. It turned out that the bet stood, but Vernons Pools objected to his winning, saying it was a certainty that he would win and therefore not a fair gamble. They won their case and Dennis lost.

He may have been safe from the war in Wombourne, but living with us had tricky moments for young Billy. This incident sticks in my mind when Billy was around five or six. It was a cold, wintry day and Billy was sitting on a small green stool in the living room, close to the fire. Suddenly, it seemed, he began to cry.

'Whatever's wrong with you?' stormed Mom, who'd just come into the room.

'I'm burning,' said Billy. With that, Mom gave him a clout that knocked him off the stool. Needless to say, he never sat too close to the fire again.

Mom was a hard taskmistress, and if you misbehaved or she felt you hadn't used common sense and so had done something silly or thoughtless, then you'd feel the back of her hand. I didn't like it – of course I didn't. But I accepted this was how it was. Mom didn't just hit us behind the closed doors of Common Road. Once, we were in Woolworths in Wolverhampton. There was something I wanted, and I was stamping my feet and having a tantrum when Mom said that I couldn't have it. Then she gave me a clout around the ears.

'Good God, look how the boy is crying,' another woman in the store said to Mom. It's clear to me now that this other woman was shocked at what Mom had done. But Mom wasn't remorseful at all. 'The more that comes out of his eyes, the less it will come down his legs,' was her very blunt reply.

As well as taking whatever punishments came your way, you also learnt never to complain to Mom of any ailments, especially stomach ache. If you did, it was upstairs to the bathroom and the dreaded 'enema', which was a bowl of hot soapy water and a simple pipe that was pushed up your backside, a bulb in the centre and the other end of the pipe in the bowl of soapy water, and squeezed. Not nice at all.

The other method that Mom used on all three of us boys was a dose of syrup of figs. She called the dose a 'jollop' and I loathed the thick, foul-tasting potion. I remember once being in Oakes's shop in the village centre to buy a bottle, and as Mrs Oakes handed it to me, I threw up all over the sweets displayed on the counter. Just the look of the bottle was enough, never mind having to swallow the contents!

In a bid to outsmart us when she didn't have any syrup of figs, Mom used to split a Black Jack sweet and put inside some Beechams Powders called State Express (another traditional stomach upset remedy). Finally, there came the day when Larry had had enough. As us three boys lined up to receive our dose of syrup of figs, Larry knocked the spoon and its contents out of Mom's hand. She was so shocked, she didn't retaliate and I cannot remember ever having to endure the concoction again.

Whilst she could be strict with us, Mom was equally fierce if she thought anyone had done any of us a wrong turn. One day, several years before I started school, Larry and Irwin were late home from Wombourne Primary School. They told her it because their teacher, Mr Corrigan, had made them go to the village hall to pick up all the bits of food that were on the floor after the children's lunch was held there. (We would walk from school down the low valley along to the village hall for lunch.)

Mom was furious. She went to the school early the next morning and she grabbed him – physically grabbed him – in the playground and was giving him hell until the headmaster,

Mr Johnny Apse, rushed into the playground and told her to stop.

'Gladys! Stop it. I will deal with the problem,' he said.

'No child of mine should be picking up bits of food,' she insisted. She felt that her children being made to pick up other people's food scraps was comparable to being abused. It was ironic that, by the time they went to secondary school, Mr Corrigan had also switched to become a secondary school teacher. Apparently, he asked my brothers not to mention the incident with Mom.

Mom's aggression reared its head again in what she saw as defence of Irwin. The Middle 'Un had been on a coach going to secondary school when the coach passed a cyclist. Irwin had put his hand out through the coach window to take this bloke's cap off his head. He'd then thrown it back out into the hedge, a few yards along. The next day, the cyclist was waiting for the Middle 'Un at the coach stop – and whacked him around the head. When Irwin told Mom, she was livid. The following morning, she stood at the bottom of our drive waiting for the cyclist to come past. When he did, she pulled him off his bike and roughed him up. Jack Gash, the local policeman, stopped by that day, too (quite possibly also on his bike), and gave Mom a police warning.

Another time, Mom had a spat with our neighbours. The Caswell's house was divided from ours by the driveways, and the problem started when Mom said that Joe Caswell had thrown a dead rat over the fence from their garden into ours. Mom chucked it right back, and the toing and froing of this rat went on for several days until Mom had a go at Joe. A loud exchange of words followed with the final exchange.

Mom: 'Don't throw that stinking rat over here again.'

Joe: 'Arsehole.'

Mom: 'Yes, you've got one. Just below your nose.'

Mom's temper was an unpredictable constant in my childhood. It didn't ruin it; I would say I had a wonderful childhood. Mom looked after us thoroughly in her way, by which I mean she fed us and kept us clean. For example, she would always get meals and drinks ready, right to having a cup of tea for each of us set out on the table. I have an early memory of looking through the handrails on the stairs to see if my tea was on the table before I came down in the morning. If it wasn't, which was rare, I would throw a right 'Benny' and my two brothers would tease me for getting into a flap.

Of course my childhood generally would have been smoother if Mom had been calm more of the time. I am aware that she carried her own sadness in that when I was around two or three years old she gave birth to another child, who was stillborn. Once, I overheard her talk about it to another woman, describing the scars from the caesarean section on her stomach as a result of that tragic birth as 'Jacob's ladder'. I knew from a different conversation overheard some years later that it had been another boy.

Another incident I remember with Billy Riley was when we were watching a Wombourne football team playing at Rookery Road pitch. Billy came to Mom and me and in his hand he had a few rabbit droppings. He must have picked them up. He asked Mom what they were and Mom said they were currants. He went to put them in his mouth, but Mom did stop him from doing so.

One of the saddest things in relation to Mom's tendency to be cruel was when I found out that she had drowned our cat, Minnie Mow, in the large water butt that stood at the back of the house and was always full of rainwater falling from the roof. The cat had canker in her ears. Treatable, but people like us didn't go to the vet in those days. So Mom had decided to kill the cat, just like that.

Even though he might not have considered taking the cat to the vet either, I know Dad would have had no part in this cruel type of affairs. Certainly, Dad never put a finger on any of his children. In fact, I don't think he ever even raised his voice at us. Outside of the family, too, he was known for being quiet and was well respected in the local community. As well as volunteering to be a cricket umpire, he was a fair snooker player and also helped to build the Civil Defence Club.

I can't remember him playing football, but he did have a medal of some kind for playing football for Wombourne in the amateur league. The pitch was off Rookery Lane, not far from where he lived on Common Road. A lot of Wombourne's middle class lived on Rookery Lane, as did a few of the rich people, who also lived on the Green Hill Road, which ran from Lower End to the main road that linked Himley to the right and Wolverhampton to the left.

It was at Lower End, close to a cottage that belonged to Clara Bow, that I would see an old guy wearing a straw hat and leaning on a walking stick as he sat by the house. For hours he'd sit there! Perhaps he watched the swallows nesting in the cottage outhouses, as they did each year. As a young child who was always on the move, his stillness caught my eye.

A mild-mannered man, I remember Dad holding me on the saddle of his motorbike when it was parked on the drive. When he came home from work, I would wrap myself around his leg, with my feet on his feet, and he would walk us around the house – through from the kitchen into the front room and even up the stairs to the two bedrooms and box room! Once, Larry gave Dad a pretend haircut, which ended with Dad's hair getting burnt. In those days, the barber would finish the cut by singeing the hair at the back of the neck, as it was believed to prevent colds. On this day, after pretending the comb was scissors, Larry used a piece of paper that he'd lit from the fire to 'singe' Dad's hair, only it caught fire and the three of us patted Dad's head and the flames stopped. Even then, Dad didn't shout. Amazing.

The biggest thing in my dad's life was his obsession with fishing, and that rubbed off on all of us boys. Dad's best friend, Arthur Day, lived at Battlefield Terrace, another arm of Wombourne. I remember Arthur calling most Sundays to take Dad fishing. Arthur had a small white van and they would drive to the Wombourne Canal or Patshull Pool, at a village called Pattingham, a few miles from Wombourne. I can see Dad holding up a pike he has caught. To me as a tiny child, that pike seemed as long as the length of our kitchen doorway! Dad didn't eat the pikes he caught, but gave them to a Polish man at Ferro Enamels who liked them.

During my earliest years, our weeks tended to have a bit of a routine, even to what we ate. On Sundays, there would be tinned pears with bread and butter for tea – this was seen as a treat. We also had sliced onions and cucumber soaked in vinegar eaten with plenty of bread and butter.

Mom was a good cook and, again on Sundays, she would make a cake using a big yellow mixing bowl that I was allowed to scrape clean so that I could eat the uncooked but very sweet cake mix. There was no fridge, just a pantry area two steps down from the kitchen with a shelf that housed a 'meat safe' – a large, netted contraption which held the fresh food. It was free from flies and out of the sun, but it was also at room temperature.

Living in the countryside meant that we didn't go hungry. We grew vegetables (and had some that Mom's parents and Arthur got from the gardens where they worked). In summer, rows of raspberry canes hung heavy with fruit. For meat, we ate rabbit. There was a saying, 'Only eat rabbits when there is an R in the month', which meant we only had from May until August without them (this was the rabbits' breeding season). This was tolerable because there were more fresh vegetables and fish during the summer.

Sometimes, if the harvest was early, we'd break the rule and also have rabbit in August. As the combine harvester reaped the corn, rabbits would run out, only to be shot by farmworkers or chased by us children. At the end of harvesting, the dead rabbits would be lined up – there could be more than 200 of them. The downside of rabbits was preparing them for cooking, a process known as 'paunching'. The smell was gross. It would also stay with the one who did the paunching, because when they farted, the smell was the same. We also ate rooks, but only about once a year when dozens of birds would be needed to create an enormous pie that would be shared by the extended family.

Whilst she cooked, Mom sang along to the radio and she had a nice singing voice. The radio was powered by a battery called an accumulator that had to be taken to a shop called Denscam's where it would be swapped for a fully charged one when it was getting low on power. I'd say the radio was one of a few little 'luxuries' our family had. At all times, I was conscious that money was tight. It was the same for most of our neighbours and it bred a culture where people would be prepared to do unpleasant tasks or things that were simply horrible, because they needed the money. Mom, for instance, killed chickens – our own chickens, which we kept in a pen at the bottom of our long garden – and the fowl neighbours would bring for her to wring their necks. Far worse was the behaviour of a guy who lived in Rookery Lane and kept pigeons in his loft. Now and again, keeping the birds here would lead to rats and this man would then agree to bite a live rat's neck to kill it if someone gave him 2 *s.* and 6 *d.* to watch him do it, which they did. Truly, Wombourne in the 1940s was a different world from today.

Lots of women from Common Road went potato picking each summer, including Mom. They would take their children with them (obviously I would go along), some of whom were still in prams. Everyone would take a bottle of tea and a separate bottle of milk; there were no flasks in those days. One year, I remember that there was a woman from Red Hill Avenue (her husband was a policeman) who had her baby in a pram. Suddenly, the baby started screaming. It turned out the baby had taken what it thought was a swig of tea but had turned out to be vinegar. The woman had taken the wrong bottle from the table at home. That same year, one of the potato pickers was a German ex-prisoner of war. When he snapped that all Englanders were pigshit, Mom answered, 'Yes, and Germans are bullshit and we made you run.'

Mom was an out-and-out Tory. She adored Winston Churchill. Years later, when he came back into power in 1951, Mom, who had been listening to the radio, came up the stairs shouting, 'We are in. We are in.'

No one knew who my dad voted for. He never told anyone.

Blackpool was the only place we ever went to for a holiday as a family. We always stayed at the same guest house, taking the train from Wolverhampton Low Hill Station to Preston, Lancashire, and then changing for Blackpool. This particular day was probably in around 1946. Field Marshall Montgomery (the commander of the Eighth Army during the war) was parading through the seaside town, and Mom hated him.

Why?

As I have mentioned, her brother Arthur was in the Irish Fusiliers and Monty, as he was popularly known, was their leader. One day during the war, he had told a group of soldiers that if they could cross a swollen river he would give them each a pack of cigarettes. Arthur was one of those soldiers but he couldn't swim. He made it, presumably with help from his comrades. But to Mom what Montgomery said to the troops was reckless and stupid.

I don't know where Dad or my brothers were, as there was just Mom and I at the side of the road when Montgomery came into view. The celebrated commander acknowledged the cheers of the crowds who had gathered on the streets of Blackpool by saluting as he stood in the back of an army jeep. As he got near to us, Mom stared right at him and said, 'Monty, you bastard.'

The look on his face was one of disbelief, but Mom's face showed satisfaction. She had done what she had set out to do!

On another trip to Blackpool, the Middle 'Un nearly got left behind at a connecting station. He'd gone to buy sweets from a platform shop, when we all got onto the train. The doors were closed and a station worker picked him up and shoved him through the window and onto the train just as it began to pick up speed. For years, I had nightmares about this moment.

When I was five, I followed my brothers to Wombourne Primary School, but it made few impressions on me. I liked the mile-long walk to school and recall seeing mice chase through the grain barns on my route. But I can't recall much of those early lessons or learning to read and write, except always struggling to spell 'Saturday' and putting an 'e' instead of a 'u'. I do remember fighting in the playground. Not me – I stayed well clear of trouble as Robert Beddle and Panda Spillar battled it out for four nights on the trot. Even at primary age, I had learnt that the wise move is to steer clear of arguments if you can.

3: SNICK AND THE GREAT OUTDOORS

Amongst the very best bits of fortune in my childhood was that my best friend lived just three doors down at number 12. Terry Stone. Always called Snick because he made a soft *snick, snick* sound with his tongue on the roof of his mouth, he was my best friend right through boyhood and I am still in touch with him today. Like me, Snick still works. He is the caretaker at a complex of flats in Dudley where he lives with his partner of many years.

That reminds me of a funny joke I know about Dudley: 'Excuse me, is there a B&Q in Wolverhampton?' said a motorist to a guy walking down the road in Wolverhampton. The guy thought about it and replied, 'No. But there are two D's in Dudley.'

My carefree days spent with Snick truly were the best days of my early life.

Snick's dad, Stan, had died in Burma (now Myanmar) when Snick was five years old. Stan had been shot by a Japanese sniper during the Second World War and this had a big effect on Snick. His mum, Kate, did all she could to care for Snick and his older brother, Roy. She worked as a cleaner in Lily Crowe's shop but struggled to provide enough to feed and keep both boys. As a child who had lost his father in the war, Snick was given a place at the Royal Wolverhampton Orphanage. He boarded there, too, returning to his family home only for the long summer holidays and Christmas and Easter.

Snick was a year older than me, but you wouldn't know it. We both wanted to get up to just the same sort of mischief.

Snick and I were both drawn to wildlife. Many times that was a good thing, and indeed those early years discovering nature have led to my lifelong passion for wildlife in general and birds in particular. But on occasions, how I behaved towards living creatures was less good. I was unthinkingly cruel, in the way that young children can sometimes be. To give an example, the fowl pen at the end of our garden backed on to a field owned by Bob Hodges, who kept cows on it. Now and again, Snick and I would climb over the latch gate into the field and then set mousetraps on the back of our fowl pen so that we could catch sparrows, which then died in our traps. It wasn't frowned on back then – farmers disliked sparrows because they would eat their corn crops. Nevertheless, I regret it now.

Other times, Snick and I were just typical cheeky boys. We'd pull up and eat horseradish in Rookery Road (it was so sharply hot on the tongue!). We'd tease Lily's husband, Frank Crowe, who'd lost a thumb in an accident at the shop when a huge block of ice severed it. We would look at him and stick our thumbs up. We would also call the postman Tick-Tock as he rode by on his bike.

We'd also be first in line whenever my neighbour-but-one, Mr Fox, killed one of his pigs, which he did in his back garden, and for a specific reason.

Mr Fox ran the butcher's shop in the village, so this was a fairly regular event. You couldn't miss the commotion of killing a pig, as it was so loud. Having its throat cut would make any animal squeal. Snick and I made sure we were around when the slaughter took place, because we needed the pig's bladder. We would blow it up with a bike pump, tie it up with cord and then that would be our football for kicking about in the street for about two or three hours before it burst! Sounds crazy, but in those days kids like us certainly did not have the money to buy real footballs. Just about anything would be kicked about instead, including pigs' bladders.

In the summer months, Mr Fox and his butcher's shop was also handy for another reason. In a large shed to the rear, Mr Fox would keep meat waste hanging up. Under this waste was a large dish, and in the dish were the large maggots that had fallen from the meat after the blowflies had laid their eggs. These were the best maggots you could get for fishing, and Mr Fox always let us have some.

Snick and I would spend many hours fishing on the canal at Botram Locks and Bumblehole . There's a sad story to Jimmy Sparkes's pub, which was just along by Bumblehole. My dad's brother Ernie adopted a son as a young boy and, years later, that lad came out of the pub, walked into the canal and drowned. It's believed this happened accidentally whilst he was the worse for wear through drink.

Snick and I never went more than a few miles or so from home, but we tended to take our bikes so we could explore more. It was important to watch out for horses along the canal path. These pulled the barges along the canal, most of which would be carrying coal. As soon as you saw one of these large 'heavy horses' coming towards you, you found a cut in the hedge and got into the gap! Today, there are no horse-driven barges, but you can still see the grooves on the stone bridges which the ropes attaching the horses to the boats brushed against as the horses went under the canal bridges.

One Sunday, we were playing in the brook. Because we knew it so well, we were able to keep to the shallow places, near to where two trees –'Big Tree an Little Tree' – had fallen across the water to create a pathway. Our plan was to find fish. We were looking for Red Butchers and Whiskery Dicks: real names, sticklebacks and stone loach. We were up to our shins when Alfie Hanley, who lived along Lower End, came to us all dressed up for going to church. Cheekily, we coaxed Alfie to join us by telling him that if he made it to Big Tree then he would be better than James Dyehouse. This boy was also our friend, but his dad, Sam, didn't like James playing with us. James was always timid; he never wanted to get dirty or mucky, because his dad would know he had been out with us. Egged on by this, of course Alfie, who was a couple of years younger than us, waded right into the water . . . and got his shorts soaking. I am pretty sure he didn't make church that day!

Whilst I believed in God as a boy due to Mom's instruction (and I still do believe today), going to church regularly wasn't part of my childhood.

Another quiet pastime as kids was corking. We would nail four tin tacks into the top of a cotton reel, then weave wool round the tacks, which would then grow through the centre of the reel to create a long piece of thick rope. It was a girl's pastime, but young boys would do it when bored.

This aside, Snick's and my world was almost exclusively outdoors. In particular, we became very interested in birds, to the point where we could name practically every British bird. The first time we saw a pied flycatcher was particularly spectacular. Snick and I were drawn to nests and, as it was common for children to do in those days, we took eggs. We followed the rule that we only took one egg if there were more than two in the nest. We built a collection of more than 150 bird eggs. With great care, we would blow the inside out, using the spike on a piece of hawthorn, so that we retained just the shell. I stored them at home, each one accurately named, in cotton wool in a drawer in my bedroom.

Snick and I also loved to watch the water voles. We would see them swimming from one side of the brook to the other. Everyone called them 'water rats', but they had a grace about them that you got to see if you spent time watching them as we did.

Whenever we went, we carried our catapults, which we called 'cattys'. And yes, we would shoot at most moving things, both in and out of the water. Sad but true.

We were always looking for stones that would be perfect ammo for cattys. The stones on people's drives were good. But the best of all were marbles.

Our cattys were made from a wood that formed into a fork shape. Hazel was the best wood – not easy to find in the right shape, but we persisted. Hazel also had the perfect thickness. It needed a light feel in your hand, yet to be strong too.

Once you had the 'fork', it was time to go to Fenwick's in Wolverhampton for the square elastic that we preferred. We liked it to be a quarter of an inch wide. Some 2 feet of elastic was needed, cut into two equal lengths. Next would be a leather 'tongue' cut out of an old shoe.

With all our equipment gathered together, it now needed both Snick and me to assemble the catty. First, we'd make a slight nick at half an inch down each one of the forks. This was to secure the thin cord that held the elastic to the fork. One of us would stretch and hold the elastic and the other would bind the cord and knot it tightly so that it held secure. This was repeated on the other top of the fork. The next task was to make two holes at the edge of the tongue just large enough for the elastic to go through; now the key point was to push the elastic through, making sure both ends were exactly the same length from fork to tongue. One of us would then stretch and hold the elastic after pushing about three-quarters of an inch through the holes in the tongue. Finally, the other would secure the elastic, and then we were good to go.

Our skills with cattys were second to none, I must say. Very few targets were missed. That said, my elder brother Irwin was also a good shot.

As well as shooting at them, we terrified live rats. To do this, we needed some particular equipment. Fuse wire.

I'm not proud to write this, but when we were young boys, Snick and I used to break in to one particular shed at Wombourne Sandhole to steal fuse wire. This shed had a small square window, covered up with tin rather than glass. As the smallest, I would climb in then throw the fuse wire out to Snick, who was acting as lookout.

'Somebody coming!'

I heard Snick's voice just as I was inside rooting around for the wire. In my hurry to get back I got stuck by my hip. I lost a good deal of flesh and blood that day.

So what did we need fuse wire for? To smoke out rats down by the brook. Obviously, these days when I think back, I have no idea why we wanted do this in the first place. Once you are adult, you can remember what you did as a kid, but you can't always think as that kid.

Close by the shed at Sandhole were two ponds, which were home to hundreds and hundreds of frogs. Whilst one of us held the frog by its back legs, the other would push a grass straw up its backside, blow through the straw, bend the straw over so the air would not come out too quickly, then put the enlarged frog back into the water. We found it fun to see it float across the water, doing breaststroke as frogs do, until the excess air was released and it could once again sink down into the water. But not before we had fired a few catty bricks at them.

A favourite summer day out was when we went up Green Hill then over Himley Road (it was known as Park Wall) and then continued walking for several miles until we reached Baggeridge Colliery. There would always be some sort of incident or adventure during our walks. On one occasion, we found dead guinea pigs that had been thrown over the wall. No idea why. Other times, we saw snakes basking in the sun.

We also saw weasels pursuing mice into holes along the bottom of the wall and tawny owls perching tight against the trunks of trees.

Once, we witnessed a rabbit playing dead after being pursued by a stoat. The clever rabbit got away – with its life! How many people can say they have seen that? Once, we were walking along a path separated only by wire fencing from a field belonging to Gittings Nurseries that had a bull it. Obviously, we carried our cattys with us and when the bull saw us, he charged! The animal couldn't get through the wire fence that separated us from him and so of course we were quite safe. Feeling bold, I put a marble in my catty and when he was about 10 yards away, I let fly.

The marble hit the bull square between the eyes. It looked like a scene from a comic book. It buckled at the knees and over it went, dazed. Never forget it.

What we seldom saw on our days out were other people. We were just two lads out on our own and all the happier for it. We had no mobile phones, no way to contact anyone else, but we never felt frightened or came to harm. Happy, happy days.

During term times, I used to visit Snick on Sundays. I would catch the midland red bus from Gilbert Lane opposite the Red Lion pub. It took only 15 minutes. Snick would be waiting by a back door of the school and we would walk to Penn Common and have whatever I had brought with me to eat and drink.

My favourite treat to bring was 'locust bean'. This cost half a penny a strip and was a like a broad bean, only black.

Another thing we would do when it was harvesting time was chew the corn heads continually until they were like chewing gum. You'd chew them with a polo mint and there you had it – spearmint gum!

Snick's mum's job at Lily Crowe's was handy for bonfire night. It meant we had the run of the place, sometimes before it was open. When Snick was home for half-term or the odd weekend, he and I would go into the post office area behind the counter and pick what we wanted. We would then pay for a few of the cheaper sparklers and fill our pockets with some, mostly bangers.

Penny Cannons were the best fireworks to have. We also liked 'squibs'. We used these down by the canal. One of us would hold the squib whilst the other one would light the touchpaper. When it started fizzing, we would throw it into the canal. It would look just like a submarine going under the water. We'd wait until dark to do this, when it looked particularly amazing.

The Penny Cannons were important, too, because we found a way to turn them into something far more exciting...

It took a lot of planning and skill. Snick and I would get a used-up U2 battery – the sort used then for bike lights and torches. We would carefully remove the end of the battery with a knife, then we would take out the centre and put a small hole in the side of the thin metal, just sufficiently large enough to hold a fuse. This would be removed from a Penny Cannon. Meanwhile, we would empty the gunpowder from as many Penny Cannons as needed to fill the empty battery case. Now and again, we'd drop in a few iron filings, if I had managed to sneak any away from school and the metalwork classroom. We would ram everything down in the battery case and replace the top. We used cycle insulation tape (as used on the handlebars on bikes), which we would wrap around the battery case until we were happy with the seal.

And then we had a bomb.

The first time we did this, we planted our bomb in the base of a big tree at the side of the brook. What an explosion! The tree fell into the brook and was then used for getting across to the other side. At the time, we saw no danger in this. Today you would be arrested.

Bonfire night was such a big thing in those days that the excitement began in September. A group of us would have been given the go-ahead by one person's parents that the 5th November bonfire could happen in their garden. All the kids would help with getting together old tyres and wood – anything that would burn. A guy would also have to be made, as sitting on the street with this and asking 'Penny for the guy?' really did mean that passers-by dropped a penny or so into your cap towards a fireworks fund that Lily Crowe would have unknowingly paid for.

Sometimes we had more than one guy, as there were two pubs – the Red Lion and the Vine – where collections went down very well. Two guys meant more chances to raise money! Unlike today, there were no age restrictions on children buying or letting off fireworks. Health and safety didn't get a look in.

During my early childhood, we had a small mongrel dog called Sandy Mow. Strong as an ox, he would pull Snick and me on the sledge in the snow, just like the Inuit do with their dogs. Unfortunately, we had to have him put down after he bit the paper kid.

Me and my best mate Snick, Crooked House, Himley, before it burnt down.

the cottage at the Foxhills Wombourne, part of Shaw Helliers estate, it was up this drive, where we shot the Rooks,

My Eldest brother Larry, (Bigun). Our last photo together before he passed away. Love you, Lal. RIP

my mate Snick, all of 80 yrs. and still in touch today,

4: THE DAY EVERYTHING CHANGED

The biggest sadness about my childhood is not getting to spend enough time with my dad. At first, I didn't notice that my dad was becoming gravely ill. I remember his right leg started to go on one side when he lifted it to walk. He had been seeing the doctor and was told that it was more than likely sciatica. Nothing serious. Then, I remember him going to the hospital in Wolverhampton and overhearing Mom telling a neighbour that a Professor Brodie Hughes from America was seeing my dad. Now that sounded like something! Someone from another country was taking an interest in my dad. Mom also went to see Dr Spackman, our local GP, in Wombourne one day and came back upset. Dad was home from hospital, but he wasn't really getting on with his life. He was his usual kind, gentle self with us boys, but with Mom he was quieter than ever.

I listened from the front room, then put my head by the kitchen door so that I could see them but they couldn't see me. Mom was crying, which she never did.

'What's the matter, Beck?' said Dad, using his pet name for her.

Next came words I couldn't make out, then Dad saying, 'There's no hope for me.'

It was about only two weeks after this that Dad was taken into hospital again. I can recall Mom talking to Aunt Nell next door when she returned from visiting him.

'He has a tumour on the brain. They have told me to have Ben back home, as he only has about two weeks left to live.'

Nothing hit me.

No emotion.

Nothing. Just carried on as normal.

During that fortnight, Billy Wright, the Wolverhampton Wanderers and England captain, came to see Dad. Mom, Dad and, eventually, me were fervent Wolves fans, and Dad had known Billy personally too. (Incidentally, Larry was a Notts County supporter and Middle 'Un was a West Broms fan.)

When, two weeks later on 11th July 1953, Mom came into our bedroom and told us three boys together at 2 a.m., 'Your daddy has died,' I felt the exact same nothing.

No inner emotion.

No outward tears.

I was just 10 years old. It was too much for me to process and no one in the family had the time or head space themself to help me unlock what I felt.

Incredibly, next morning whilst Mom was crying and my two brothers were also crying, I kept on with my plans. I took the bus to Wolverhampton and went to a jamboree for Scouts and Cubs held at Goodyear Tyres' grounds. I was a member of the local Cub pack at the time and loved the way it fostered teamwork and also taught you how to be more streetwise in challenging situations alongside letting you take part in outdoor activities that were great fun. I met Snick at the jamboree, of course. He was there with other kids from the orphanage.

'Dad's died,' I told him.

I don't remember his reply, only that we carried on at the jamboree, joining in with the games and trying our hand at the stalls, but it meant that Snick and I now shared a deeply sad bond. We were both young boys who had lost their dads.

I blocked out Dad's death so much that I can't remember the day of the funeral or before or afterwards. None of us boys went to the funeral.

All my memories of that time are focused on the big jamboree. So, for example, I can tell you what I won on the coconut shy that day. I was small for my age, so the stallholder said that I could come nearer to the poles. For a lad whose hobby was shooting things (with my catty), it felt easy indeed to throw a wooden ball and knock the coconut from its holder. You had five goes to try to win a coconut, but due to the stallholders' practice of using sawdust to wedge in each coconut, you had to be skilled to win. He only let me go near twice. I gave away my four coconuts.

Without Dad's wage, Mom began to really struggle for money. At one point, she wrote to one of her mum's sisters who had emigrated to Oregon, USA. She asked if she should go to America, too, to give us all a better life. But that sister wrote back to tell her that America was facing a depression and not to come. Had she said yes, what a different life I would have had. No way of knowing if it would have been better or worse, only that it would have created a different set of memories to write about now.

Mom was enterprising and thrifty and prepared to do pretty much anything. She took the view that every tiny saving counted. Take coal, for example. She would save up the slack from the coal house and put it in a sack outside. Then, when it got so cold in winter that the slack froze into cubes, she would break it up to put it onto the fire.

On top of her full-time factory job, she would help out farmers with seasonal work – from potato picking to gutting chickens and rabbits – and she also cleaned other people's houses. She skinned moles too, selling them on. I remember the skins nailed onto the shed to dry out for weeks at a stretch.

Mom also made sure that we took on part-time jobs, and from the earliest age. At some point, we all had paper rounds, picked potatoes, milked cows and did just about every type of odd farm job going. In particular, I remember spending Saturday mornings churning butter for Mrs Winnie Elliot at the farm at the Wodehouse. It would take more than two hours of turning and turning the churn handle to produce around 2 pounds of butter for the 'big house'. Every now and again, Winnie would check my work, dipping her little finger into my churning liquid and adding salt. Finally, when the glass window on the barrel was clear, she'd declare it ready to be patted. Another task was to cut the lawn edge. It was about 80 metres long . . . and I was given scissors to do it. What a chore! I was certainly younger than 11 years old and received 2 *s.* and 6 *d.*

Whilst I was butter churning or scissor snipping, the Big 'Un and Middle 'Un would cut the main lawns and milk cows as well as swill cowsheds, boil potatoes for the pigs and take the milk and cream from the farm to the big house. Now and again I would accompany them to the big house. There we would be greeted by one of Miss Shaw-Hellier's maids and told to remove our shoes and put them in the parlour. One of the maids was called Miss Partridge, known also as 'the bird'.

In addition to working on the farm, the Middle 'Un would always be on the lookout for rabbit runs, where he would set snares to catch the rabbits.

Both my brothers had paper rounds. These were big rounds, with a radius of around 8 miles or so, and they had to do them of an evening (for the evening paper) as well as at weekends. When I helped Irwin, who had the biggest round, a couple of houses stood out. Fox Hills and Hart Hill House.

On Sundays, we would make Hart Hill House our last stop. Irwin would put his two fingers in his mouth and whistle. Out would come two mongrel-like collies and off we would go, taking the shortest route to get to the railway line running from Himley to the Giggetty in Wombourne.

Another standout memory of this bit of railway line was us kids having a go on a piece of equipment called a 'boggie'. It was moved along the track by pumping a handle whilst we stood on the flat wood attached. We would take it all the way along until it would go no further, and then we would return it to its original place. Great fun.

The embankments were full of rabbits and the dogs were unreal at catching them. One of them would flush the rabbits out and the other would catch them and shake them, leaving my brother and I to pick up the carcasses. We could have four or five in one afternoon. Mom would have one and the rest would be given to neighbours.

Fox Hills - situated just after the Red Lion pub on the Wolverhampton to Himley Road – had a drive about 400 metres long with a lodge at the road end. It was unique (then) for having iron railings (which are still there today), as most houses had their railings taken down to be used in the manufacture of weapons for the Second World War.

Fox Hills was also home to a husky dog. It would not move when we went up the drive, but on the way back we had to really go very quickly past on our bikes, as it would then chase us all the way down. Nasty piece of work, that dog.

A happier memory relating to the same house was when I went with Uncle Arthur in quest of our rook pie. There were lots of tall trees to the left-hand side of the Fox Hills drive where rooks tended to nest. All this land and houses belonged to Miss Shaw Hellier. In spring, there would be perhaps 50 or 60 nests. Uncle Arthur would take two guns for each of us to shoot the branchers – this was the name for the young rooks who had left their nests and would be perched on tree branches close by. We would use a .177 cadet major pellet gun, which would inflict less damage. We needed the intact thighs and breasts of about 18 to 20 birds to make one pie.

To earn a bit more money, Mom took in two lodgers: Ron Corbett and Tom Smith, nicknamed Tiger. They both worked nights in a factory, C & B Smith, which was an iron foundry in Wolverhampton. And they were both Welsh, from Port Talbot.

Ron was a dreadful man. He was dour and left the house in such a mess. As the youngest, I was home first from school. It got to the point where all I was doing was clearing up after him so that it would look OK before Mom came in from work. I told Mom that he had to go. Sure enough, she told him to leave. Tom stayed and he went on to become Mom's partner. He was a married man, and when his wife came unannounced to our house she was so angry that she threw her wedding ring into our back garden. Mom found it and sold it.

One night, Mom went with Tom to the Grand Theatre in Wolverhampton to see Bob Monkhouse. Bob asked the audience if anyone was out with the lodger. Mom and Tom went on stage and Bob presented Mom with a top-of-the-range handbag. I liked Tom a good deal; in fact, I feel grateful to him. He and Mom moved to Hastings in 1958 and, as the years went on and Mom developed Parkinson's disease, he continued to care lovingly for her until her death in 1974. By this time, they had moved back to Wombourne. Mom was aged only 64 years and seven months. I do regret now that when Mom first showed the effects of Parkinson's but it had yet to be diagnosed, I used to shout at her when her hands shook. How could I have been so cruel?

Isn't it true in life that as you get older, you also get kinder and more tolerant? That said, I have a hunch that one day, when I join Mom upstairs, she will greet me with a clout around my ears!

I would say I have always had Mom's resourcefulness. Just as Mom would take on a hundred and one tasks if she could earn a few shillings, as a boy, I tried different things to earn a bit of cash.

Now and again Snick and I would see a man we called 'Soldier Jim' walking from Red Hill Avenue and then along Common Road. It was now around 1948, yet he still wore his army uniform and had kept it smart. On a couple of occasions, as he drew near, we would get down on our hands and knees and pretend we were looking for something. Sure enough, Soldier Jim would ask us what were we looking for.

'We've lost our sixpence,' we would say, trying to sound downcast. Without hesitation he would put his hand in his pocket and give us 6 *d*. On reflection, he more than likely knew that we were telling a lie, but he never said anything.

We coined a different way to make cash at phone boxes. In those days, public telephone boxes had an A and B button. When you needed to make a call, you would put money in first, ring the number and then, if the call was answered, you had to push button A for them to hear you. If it wasn't answered, you pushed button B to get your money back. We rigged up a phone box using a concealed Woodbine packet. When button B was pressed, the money would go into our Woodbine packet! We would collect it after the caller had given up on getting their money back. Not a lot of money, but every little helped.

We'd spend the money from these schemes on sweets mainly, but sometimes we'd opt for a couple of Woodbine cigarettes. Joe Abbis, who had a little shop in the village and was also the local coalman, had no hesitation in selling them to us, despite our age.

The fags were always 'for someone else'.

For ourselves, we smoked nub ends, picking them off the road. There were no filters in those days, so a discarded fag had a nice bit of tobacco in it. We would unravel them and put the baccy in a Horlicks tin to be smoked in an acorn.

It was almost as complicated a procedure as creating the cattys.

We'd collect acorns in the autumn and hollow them out (ready to fill with tobacco) and then make a small hole in the side, just large enough to fit a piece of straw. This could be a hollow grass stem that would be about 8 inches long. It needed to be that length because as you smoked your acorn pipe, the grass would burn down. Our only expense was the matches.

Everybody seemed to smoke back in those days, except Mom. Dad had been a Woodbines man and my brother Irwin used to smoke Typhoo Tea that he rolled up in a newspaper. I remember it stank to high heaven. He must have been only seven or eight when he began doing it.

In summer Snick and I smoked what we called 'Pug Wuff'. It grew on the side of the road and it went brown in the summer. I've got no idea where we got the name from, but the source was a leaf a little like a chrysanthemum leaf. When you put these leaves in the palms of your hands and rubbed them, they disintegrated into small bits that you could put in the acorn pipe. Again, the smell was unique.

Despite playing with fire – literally, in the case of those home-made bombs and fireworks – Snick and I came to harm only a very few times.

On one occasion, we were larking about at the brook using a strong branch from a tree, a straight piece. We used it like a pole vault. Once, I went over the top of the branch to land on the opposite bank on my knee. I felt a sharp pain and I looked down and saw a deep cut in my knee. Snick got out his hanky and pressed hard, but nothing was going to stop the blood. Luckily, Mom was in when we raced back home and she took me to Dr Spackman, who put two stitches on the wound. I believe the instrument he stitched it with was sitting on the side in a jar of methylated spirits before he plunged it into my leg!

I still have the scar today, on the left-hand side of my left knee.

Another time, the Middle 'Un and I were round at Snick's. I thought I would scare him by firing my catty at a piece of corrugated tin that was patching up his fence. The noise would be tremendous. As it was, instead of scaring Snick, the marble from my catty hit him in the right eye. We raced over to where his mum was working at Lily Crowe's shop and someone took him to Wolverhampton Eye Infirmary. He had a detached retina and stayed in hospital for a week. I remember the date he came out: 6th September, on his birthday. That put paid to cattys for a while, but thankfully not our friendship.

Whilst giving cattys a rest, we developed Dutch arrows. We used a small bamboo cane with a nail pushed into one end and the opposite end split twice so that a piece of cardboard could be inserted to create a dart capable of flight. We used a piece of string with a knot at one end that we would put along the bamboo.

It was brilliant fun. With practice we were able to send our darts well over 100 metres.

I can't remember whose idea it was to take a fully fledged jay to have as a pet. We found him in a tree and he was kept in Snick's fowl pen at the top of the garden. We named the bird Charlie. He was let out in the day to fly free, but every evening he would return. It lasted for a few special months, then he disappeared. We assumed he'd flown off, but then discovered that some kids from Red Hill Avenue had killed him.

It was very rare that you saw other races of people when I was a young child. I do remember the first people I saw who looked different to me, and I was frightened of them. I was playing on the street in Common Road when I spotted two men wearing turbans, each carrying a suitcase. I got behind a small wall that ran along the road by Billy Lamb's field. I felt sure that as they passed me they would have heard my heart thumping! Mom told me later that they were door-to-door salesmen from a cleaning products company called Clean Easy and there was nothing to worry about. By the mid 1950s, Wolverhampton had become home for a good number of Jamaican immigrants – the Windrush generation.

I remember seeing a piece in the Wolverhampton *Express & Star*. The MEB engineers had been doing some work on the big green distributors that were on the pavements. These were large metal electricity storage units used in those days. Inside these distributors, they found a pile of letters. It was discovered that some of the immigrants thought that they could post them in there by slipping them under the top covers. Also during this time of early migration, there would be at least double the amount of residents in the houses. To make it work, half of them worked nights and the other half days. They also had cars. Tiger told me that one month everyone would give money to one person and that would be the deposit for the car, then the next month someone else would get it. Clever eh?

Nearly half a century later, of course, I would warmly welcome my son's African wife into our family.

When he was around 12 years old, the Middle 'Un was a paper boy for Lily Crowe. I remember being in the shop and Lily went to get the newspapers for him from the post office part of the shop. Whilst she was out of sight, my brother grabbed a handful of sweets from the counter and put them in his pocket. Lily then brought out the newspapers and off we went. But when he then said to me, 'Here, have a sweet,' I said, 'No, and I'm going to tell Mom!'

I used this as a form of blackmail for about a year; for example, when he went off to play with the Red Hill kids and said Snick and I couldn't come, I would say that I would tell Mom about the sweets. So he'd change his mind and let my friend and I join in.

At 11 years old, I joined Kingswinford Secondary School, where Mr Bowers was headmaster. It wasn't an important part of my life and I knew from the outset that I wouldn't be there long enough to sit any O-levels. Both my brothers had left before I arrived. Larry's first job was working down the pit and Irwin was a pen-pusher, as clerks were known in those days.

For the first few weeks of term, the teachers assumed that I would be very bright like Irwin. In fact, I was more middling than the Middle 'Un. I got a B in most classes.

I was a good long-distance runner and one year I made the final of the mile race. I was second favourite to win, against Panda Spillar. Nearing the end of the race, I could see that I still had enough energy in me to sprint the last yards and take the prize, but I didn't push forwards. I remembered those fights I had witnessed, but not joined in with, during my primary school years. It was not worth the risk of Panda giving me a thump because he hadn't won. Sometimes in life it is better to think of the longer-term consequences!

I understood the need for English and maths, of course I did, but I couldn't see the point of music or RE lessons. My passion in school was for 'nature studies'. We'd go for walks in Kingswinford Park. One day, a kid called Ernie Crank (who had this cruel nickname because his nose was lopsided and his ears were funny) shouted, 'There's a bird,' and produced a catapult from his pocket. He fired a brick at the bird. The teacher went berserk.

Each day, I made the 5-mile journey to school at Pensa Street, Kingswinford, on board a Noakes coach. Often, I sat next to Ray Woodhall, who lived in Battlefield Terrace. His dad was a budgerigar breeder and I paid 10s. (50p) to him for a green budgie we called Joey that went on to live for 18 years.

The money I used had come from Mom's widow's pension, which I always picked up at Lily Crowe's on Mom's behalf, as she could never get there herself due to working such long hours at the die-casting factory.

Sometimes Larry would give me 2 *s.* to take to school to buy some sweets from the tuck shop near the school. There was no need for dinner money. As a child without a dad, I qualified for free school dinners.

A standout incident for me was when Ray and I were collecting empty milk bottles. We were the milk monitors for the school, and doing this job excused us from assembly. Every child received milk, and by late in the day, you had to look right through the school for the empties. They would wind up under the stage, in corners of the assembly hall and so forth. Once, the caretaker asked us what we were doing. Whilst we told him the truth, he then reported back to the woodwork teacher that we had been smoking underneath the school stage.

This led to one of only two times that I got the cane at school. The next day, Ray and I were given four strokes on our hands by the woodwork teacher, Charlie Ward. When we were in our next lesson, our regular class teacher saw how distressed we were. We explained what had happened and he was furious. I believe he went and pushed that teacher up against a wall and told him that he must never hit 'his' children again.

The second time I received the cane, and this time was one stroke, was from Mr Skillbeck, the metalwork teacher, for hitting match-heads with a hammer on the anvil – it was the smell that gave me away.

I remember another lad getting a smack from the English teacher, Miss Derry. She sat on a desktop without realising this meant she also showed a bit of her thighs. A kid called Carpenter, who thought himself a bit of a lad and had his hair cut into a 'Tony Curtis' style, gave a wolf whistle. That was it! The young new teacher jumped down from the desk and gave Carpenter a smack so hard you would have thought she wanted to knock his head off his shoulders. Needless to say, no call-outs or comments ever came her way again.

I've mentioned already how Mom had no qualms about killing chickens – she needed the money. She was paid to do so by a Mr Farmer, who kept a coop in his gardens. He also sold eggs. One Saturday morning, this man's son Geoff arrived with a cockerel for Mom to kill, only Mom was out shopping.

'Mom's not here, Geoff,' Larry said, 'but I am sure we can do it together.'

Geoff held the cockerel under his armpit and Larry got its head twisted and pulled at the same time he must have done something else, but I am not sure what, as the cockerel's head came off. Geoff dropped it in shock and the cockerel ran very briefly around with no head on, and its head was jumping up and down on the drive. No idea how, but it must have been nerves.

Mom went mad. But Geoff didn't get in trouble as Mom simply plucked and dressed the chicken, so the cockerel went back, oven-ready, with Mr Farmer none the wiser.

A few years after Dad died, I remember the headline on the front of the Wolverhampton *Express & Star*: 'Wombourne widow fined £50'.

The story was about Mom.

The backstory was that when Larry left school, Mom had him working down the pit digging coal. She wanted him to do this because at that time this particular job meant you could avoid being called up for two years of National Service, which all young men had to do through the late 1940s and into the 1950s once they reached 18.

Essentially, it was all about money. Mom relied on a share of Larry's wage to support the family. There was also the bonus that working in the pit meant the family received a ton of coal each month for a very small fee. If we had enough coal, Mom would sell it. You could have it delivered to another address for a small fee. If our coal ran out, Mom would pull hedge stakes up out of hedges along Common Road and use the wood as kindling. policeman Jack Gash would give Mom many warnings about it but when you had to wait until you could afford bags of coal, it was the only way to keep warm in the winter.

One day my brother went to Wolverhampton and signed up to the army anyhow. The first Mom knew of it was when an officer came to our door one evening to tell her that her son had signed to join the 16/5th Queen's Royal Lancers. Larry went to Catterick for training, then to Germany. I recall Mom being worried when Larry was patrolling the Soviet/Hungarian border during some uprising. He was now a tank commander.

When her second son was nearing 18, Mom was desperate to avoid the same happening again. She went to a tribunal to try to keep Irwin out of the army, pleading that, with no husband, she needed Irwin as a wage earner. She lost the tribunal and – far worse – it emerged that she hadn't been declaring all her earnings. She was fined the £50 for failing to declare her 10 s. a week widow's pension to her bosses at the die-cast factory.

Mom was so ashamed, she didn't leave the house for a long time. It took our lovely next-door neighbour, whom I knew as Auntie Edna, to encourage her to go out again.

Irwin joined the Royal Army Medical Corps – the 'scab and matter boys', as Uncle Arthur called them. He also called them, 'rob all my comrades'.

Arthur had been a stretcher-bearer himself during the war. He had been captured in Italy during the Second World War, near to Mount Etna. Arthur's unit were dug in to a trench and had captured one German soldier, whom they had in there with them. There was a gap in the ridge and the captured man was able to shout out to a larger group of other Germans across the ridge.

Those other Germans then came over because their captured comrade had told them that he was being held by only six English soldiers. Arthur and the other five English squaddies were captured and put into a prisoner of war camp in Germany until the end of the war.

By the time of my final day at school, the month before my 15th birthday, both my brothers were away and there was just Mom, Tom, me and Sandy Mow at home. I remember the teacher asking me to stand up and say where I was going to work.

'At Wodehouse in Wombourne. In the gardens or on the farm,' I said confidently. It was, of course, what my uncle and my grandfather and my great-grandfather would have said had they been asked, so it felt perfectly OK to say the same. In truth, I didn't rightly know – but there was no way I was going to say that!

Mom (head scarf) and Dad behind at Wembley, FA Cup Final 1949, 3-1 to the Wolves. The only photo I have of them.

Again last picture of Larry, with Beryl. He loved Bear Lamb. Miss you, Bigun. RIP.

Dave Wild, with Steve and Beryl in the Gambia. RIP Dave. Lovely memories.

Steve (butter wouldn't melt!). Curlew Rd, Heron Park, Gloucester.

5: ROARING THROUGH MY TEENAGE YEARS

I have named this chapter with reference to the powered vehicles I had and loved once I was 16. Whilst I went on to have a BSAC12 motorbike with a respectable 250cc engine, my first vehicle was a motorised bike that was more like a moped. I shared it with my brother Larry. Our arrangement was that he would have the 'Zundap' at nights and I would use it to get to my job with Pearks, now at Bilston.

One evening in 1958, I was returning from the Wellington, Shropshire, Pearks store where I was helping out, when the motorbike broke down at Burnhill Green. Luckily, I spotted a phone box, but I couldn't remember the full home phone number because Mom and I had recently moved to 206 Warstones Road in Penn. I knew only that the number ended in 6. I paid two pence to ring the operator and asked for the number for 'Guest, 206 Warstones Road'. But the number given didn't end in 6.

'No, that's not it,' I said.

Next, I heard him say to his colleague: 'We have a nutter in a phone box who asked for a number and has now said I have given him the wrong one!'

I stuck with my request, though, and the next number he offered did end in 6. I rang Mom, who organised for Larry to come towards Burnhill Green whilst I pushed the motorbike towards Penn. Some 90 minutes later, we met. I was sweating like a pig due to pushing the bike all this time. Larry? He fixed the bike in minutes. A bare wire had touched the frame under the saddle, and he expertly taped it up. Problem solved. No wonder I always said that if I was on a desert island, the one person I would choose to be with me would be the Big'Un!

I enjoyed my work at Pearks right from the start. Each day was very busy. For example, over Easter 1958 the store in Queen's Street sold over 10,000 pounds of bacon! My first time serving on the provisions counter was a day I'll never forget. The till at that time was simply a wooden drawer with compartments, which was attached under the counter. It held all the different coins – ha'pennies, pennies, tanners, bobs, two bobs, half-crowns – and notes from nickers (10 s.) through to fivers. There were very few five-pound notes in those days. They were white, about 8 inches by 5 inches in size. No one told me that you had to take care as you opened the drawer. I had just made my first sale and pulled it open confidently . . . and the entire contents went onto the floor.

Picking it all up took ages, not least because I had to clear each coin free from sawdust. Yes – no smooth, smart flooring in those days. The floor behind the counter consisted of wooden boards, and the sawdust was thrown down each evening to stop staff from slipping on the boards. I made another simple error when I sold my first sausages. I put them loose onto greaseproof paper and passed them straight to the customer.

'Would you mind putting them into a bag,' I was told politely.

Pearks was part of the Allied Suppliers Group. In the late 1950s, ASG was on every high street – there were more than 3,000 stores – trading under the names Lipton, Home & Colonial, Maypole and, of course, Pearks. In Scotland, the name on the facia was Galbraith's.

Despite being the same company, competition was fierce. Pearks's slogan was 'the store that never sells a bad egg', and to make sure that this held true, whenever a customer asked for eggs, each and every one was 'candled'. This involved putting each egg to be sold into a box with six holes at the top. Inside the box was a light bulb which would be switched on to check for any 'darkening' on an egg. This darkening would only happen if an egg had become old; a new, fresh egg would stay clear under the bright light.

What a lot of work for a few eggs! All the eggs that passed were put into double paper bags, one by one, to give them the best chance of not getting cracked on their journey back to the customer's house.

Our store had two Berkel bacon machines, one manual and one electric, plus a cooked meats machine. Elsie Ramsbottom trained me on the bacon side and Dorothy Bradley on cooked meats.

Bacon – up to 120 sides of it – was delivered weekly to the store on a Pickford's flatback lorry. Driver Paddy used to talk to me about surviving the Dunkirk evacuation during the Second World War. We took the bacon from the lorry in a hessian sack, which was then slung over our shoulder to make carrying the very heavy sides of bacon round to the back of the shop slightly easier. Even so, at just 4 feet 8 inches and slim, it was a real struggle for me.

There were no cold rooms in those days and you could only fit so much into the store's fridges.

The sides of bacon were stacked on a Formica board, three one way and three the other way. Elsie, Dot and myself would bone out all the sides of bacon. After training, I could (and still can even today) bone out a side of bacon in about 4 minutes.

Sometimes bacon that had to be left out would be affected by blowflies and then maggots. This would be rectified by wiping the bacon with a cloth soaked in vinegar. The cheeses, butter and fats fared better: they were stored in an underground cellar that was naturally cool.

Some customers requested home delivery for their shopping. Ernie would drive a van to their houses, or sometimes I would go out to customers' houses on a bike.

The toilets were at the back of the store, in a separate building off a passageway, and shared by workers at other shops. It was here that Stan, who worked in the printer's shop along the same passageway, would cut my hair. In return, I would 'buy' him a packet of Player's cigarettes. (In reality, it would be cigarettes that Snick had taken from Lily Crowe's shop!)

Working with Stan at the printer's was a girl with jet-black hair called Jacqueline Boden. We went many times to the pictures together. In those days, that was where courting couples went. I also made good friends with Kathleen Matthews, who had jet-black hair (again!) and the most infectious laugh, and Margaret Willets who very sadly had lost the tip of her little finger whilst operating the coffee grinder in Pearks.

Once, I went to the Odeon with both girls. In the interval, I asked if they wanted an ice cream. 'No thanks,' said Kathleen, 'I've brought this for us instead.' Out of her handbag appeared three parcels in tin foil, a lump of bread pudding inside each. Delicious!

Now and again, Snick and I would cycle to Bushbury where they lived. They were around four years older than us and it was a fantastic friendship. Eventually, both girls went to live in Cambridge and we lost touch.

Shops closed on bank holidays then and Pearks Wolverhampton used the opportunity to take their staff on an annual outing. One year it was to Aberystwyth. I was picked up by the coach at Chapel Ash and I can remember the hoorays as I got on board, all due to the black jacket with silver threads, drainpipe trousers and trendy beetle crushers shoes that I wore. My hair was 'DA' (duck's arse) style, cut into a Teddy Boy style. I did look dapper, if I say so myself!

On this trip, I again spent time with Kathleen and Margaret. Both had a habit of greeting strangers warmly, as if they knew them. The look of bewilderment on the faces of the elderly of Aberystwyth that day was something to behold!

Typical Kathleen joke: 'Could you tell me where the other side of the road is?' Then, when the elderly person would say, 'Over there,' she'd reply, 'It can't be. Someone has just sent us from over there!' Happy days.

Other Pearks girls I recall were Maureen Crocket, Nolly Noden, Yvonne, Janet, Gwyneth and Jean. Janet and I went on a good many dates. At one point, I bought her Ricky Nelson's record, *There Will Never Be Another You*. Yvonne went on to marry Dennis, a butcher from Dewhurst. But at one point she was a favourite of Mr Tustin.

Mr Tustin took a personal involvement in me, too, in that when I told him I had been prone to constipation for many years, he suggested drinking a glass of water from the hot tap – as hot as it could get – and to do this before my first mug of tea. Worked a treat.

During my apprenticeship, I went to work at different stores in and around Wolverhampton and sometimes as far afield as Wellington, Shropshire. Before I got my motorbike, I'd go by bus, train or trolley bus accordingly. At the Bilston store, I was tasked with delivering customer orders using the shop bicycle. It had a basket on the front for the groceries but was a nightmare to steer safely in poor weather or when you had to repair a puncture. Deliveries were placed in a cardboard box inside the basket. It could be packed full or, as on one occasion, just include a box of cornflakes, 2 pounds of sugar and a jelly.

Typically, I'd arrive at 6.30 a.m. to pull the blinds down outside the shop front. This was to prevent the sun making the cooked meats in the window too hot. I'd then ride the store delivery bike from the shop floor out onto the pavement around to the back of the shop, where I would begin slicing bacon and cooked meats and the very important job of dressing the front window, before the shop's opening at 9 a.m., with bacon and cold meats on one side, dry groceries on the other.

The window was the main selling point for customers, no different to a butcher's counter today. These displays would be changed every time price offers changed. I remember the Pearks own-label tea – Gold Tips – which came with perforated stamps that customers could collect and eventually exchange for teacups or even a dinner service if they drank enough tea.

One day, the store manager at Bilston, Mr Tarbuc, was called on by the manager of Jackson's, a tailor's shop next door. He wanted to know who was going to pay for his smashed window, as the lad who rode the bicycle had smashed it with his basket. It wasn't me! Fortunately, a man selling newspapers on the street outside Woolworths had seen the other lad who worked there accidentally smash the tailor's window, so no harm done.

Mr Tarbuc was a big Walsall football fan and of course I was a Wolves man through and through. We enjoyed a good deal of healthy banter on that!

At Bilston, there was an infestation of rats under the floorboards of the warehouse. I used to put a 'gin trap' down to catch them. Each morning, I'd check for any rats that were in the trap's teeth.

The saddest thing I remember about Mr Tarbuc was that he never took a holiday, always feeling he needed to be available for the store. Finally, he retired and went on holiday with his wife only to die on holiday.

By the time I was 16, I had become so reliable and effective that I was sent to help out when store managers did go away. The 'first hands' (the name given to the deputy managers) seemed pleased to see me. One time, when I picked up my wages at Pearks in Brierley Hill, the first hand said: 'Clive, I have given you an extra half a crown. That's for helping so much this week. Thank you!'

Positive customer comments came my way too. At North Street, Wellington (where I was responsible for dressing the window), I overheard someone say, 'I have been shopping here for many years and I have never seen the window look so good.'

That was when I thought to myself, *Clive, you could be quite good at this job...*

I always looked after the provisions, including ordering and the accompanying paperwork, which had names such as GR1, GR2, Section J and The Digest.

This last one was what visiting district and area managers would always ask to see. It was the store's 'Bible' and included the weekly sales performance used to calculate store managers' monthly bonuses. Section J recorded waste – dented tins and so forth. I learnt to take my time and fill these forms in accurately and neatly.

Cooked meats was an area where stores could make a few extra shillings. Jellied veal arrived in triangular 6-pound tins. When we opened these, we took care to keep the original lid. This was then placed by the meat slicing machine and every day all the trimmings or meat that were left over from slicing were put in the tin, which would then be stored in the fridge.

It might take a month before that tin became 95 per cent full, at which point you would put a complete slice of jellied veal on the top, then replace the lid. It now looked like a pristine, full tin! You would then leave this out of refrigeration for a few days, by which time it would smell somewhat. This would then be taken to the public health department, who would provide a certificate of condemnation. The certificate could then be attached to the store's Section J book for a credit from head office. This, along with putting an extra penny on the price of each customer's quarter of ham or cut of bacon, ensured you got a sales bonus every month. Happy days!

In those days, the managers' approach was that you always knew what you were making but not what you were losing. This is still the case in shops today. There weren't shoplifters, because of counter service, but managers were often unsure of how honest their staff were. So these 'tricks' were designed so that at the end of the day their figures would never be down. You had a stocktake every four weeks: a short stock result and you received no bonus.

Some of the managers in those days were real characters. I remember the chap at Pearks Tipton. He'd always say, 'Just popping out to check on Ruby.' I assumed it was an elderly friend, but found out after a few days that it was his Austin Ruby car, parked in the next street.

Aged 18, I was given the Darlaston Pearks store to manage. When I heard the news (but before I started), I went to check it out with Brian Warrington, meat area manager. Written on the window by the exiting manager was the most popular offer of the day: 'Buy two pounds of sugar, get one pound of lard free.' Only it was spelt 'shugar'! When I saw that, I knew I was set to do a better job than my predecessor. I won't name him, because we went on to become great friends when our paths crossed again later on in our retail careers.

As you'd expect for someone so young, managing my first store was a learning curve.

I remember two very sad moments from my time at Darlaston. First, a member of staff's 11-year-old son died from leukaemia. Second, after a few weeks a girl from the chemist along the street came to the back door of the store with a box that contained a litter of kittens whose mum was our store cat. I told a lad who worked at our store to get a swab (a piece of gorse cloth) and drowned the kittens. Big, big mistake. The area manager, Bill Stackhouse, had always opened a can of salmon for the kittens' mother when he visited the store. When he heard what I had done, how I kept my job, I do not know.

Behind the counter at this store was a trapdoor that led into a cellar. Staff always shouted 'trap up' to colleagues when the door was being opened, but with up to seven people working behind the counter at any one time, it was a busy, chaotic area to be. One girl, who must have not heard the call, fell into the cellar. She was shaken, but thankfully not seriously injured.

At that time, cooked meats and other counter provisions accounted for 80 per cent of the sales. Once, Mr Glanville, the district manager, told me about a corned beef and jellied veal competition. The prize for being the store that increased their sales most would be premium bonds. I hit on the idea of setting up a deal with a Parkers shop nearby. They would give us Typhoo Tea in exchange for the two cooked meats in question. With our sales boosted this way, we won the prize!

As an incentive for staff to work hard, I would offer rewards. Letting people go home early on Friday or giving them an extra afternoon off each week really made them step up the rest of the time. No wonder that practically every month I earnt a bonus on top of my £11 weekly salary.

Part of my apprenticeship involved doing a postal course – no online learning then, of course. You received tea leaves and coffee beans, amongst other items, in the post and you had to correctly identify each. I also did some training at Allied Suppliers' London head office. A complete shop was mocked up and you had to pass practical tests; for example, measuring and cutting a 90-pound Canadian cheese, complete with rind.

With the quality training I received from Mr Tustin, the tests were never a problem. Mom was sent a glowing report of my progress every six months. When I took my final exam at Wolverhampton College, I came second out of 702 people.

When not at work, I was out with Snick, who had finished school now and was back in Wombourne full-time and working at C & B Smith in Wolverhampton. We'd go fishing on free days, sometimes cycling 20 miles to Bridgenorth. We'd set off before dawn to get the best swim.

Once, I was stopped by the police for having Snick on the back of my motorbike (illegal when you were still a learner rider) and had to pay a fine in court. I was banned for six months and fined £30. Lesson learnt.

One Saturday evening, I was out with Arthur, the guy next door – Rocket Russell – and my friend Tomas. We were waiting at a bus stop for a Midland Red bus to take us home when a car pulled up behind the petrol station opposite. Three of the four men got out and began urinating against the petrol pumps.

'What do you think you're doing?' said Arthur.

'We will piss anywhere, man,' said the most striking-looking of the group. It was Mick Jagger! They were on the way back from a very early Rolling Stones gig, probably at Birmingham, and had been caught short!

I started betting on horses when I was around 16. I'd watch racing on TV and study form in the newspaper. I'd discovered I liked the thrill of winning when I was around 14 or so, through going to bingo with Mom. I had also became addicted to the 'one arm bandit' – a machine where you put a sixpence into the slot and, if a certain combination came up – Tic-Tac-Toe – then you won perhaps £20. I never got into debt over it, but I spent more on this than I should have done.

When I was around 17, I went to Jersey with Tomas and betting on horses was a big part of the fun of our trip. On the day before we flew back, I put a quid on a treble bet over three races. Little World, Hasty Nance and Dear Gazelle all won and I pocketed £37, which was half of what the two-week holiday had cost me! At the airport, I bought Uncle Arthur a watch with a black face with part of those winnings.

I'd moved in with Uncle Arthur by this time and I would stay at Wodehouse for the next 10 years. I took Joey, our budgie, with me, renaming the bird Chirvy. Arthur never married and distrusted women generally (apart from his sister, aka my mum!). He liked 'male' pursuits like shooting and fox hunting with the All Brighton Hounds and making home brew. We'd shoot together, bringing back rabbits and birds to eat for a cracking roast on Sundays with vegetables from the estate gardens and a glass from Arthur's cellar.

Arthur's house had an outside toilet – nicknamed 'the thunderbox'. Toilet paper was newspaper on a string. Oil lamps were used for lighting before electricity. Aside from a downstairs open fire, there was no heating and the bedrooms were freezing in winter. At night, I'd keep a 'cod bowl' under the bed to avoid going to the outside toilet. In winter, by morning any contents had frozen!

In those days, fresh air was considered essential for health, so even in winter, the bedroom sash window was open. I went to sleep fully dressed. I'd fixed a pull cord by my bed so I could turn on the ceiling light without having to leave my covers. One morning, three swallows had come in through the window to perch on my wire inside the bedroom, and their twittering woke me up!

Life was good with Uncle Arthur. We listened to the radio so he would know the next day's weather – essential for a gardener. We went out most evenings, and Rocket and Tomas would come along. It was always to a pub and we would take our 'snap', this being bread and cheese and black's manure (black pudding), to be eaten in the pub.

Arthur didn't say a lot, but our silence together was easy and warm. Arthur was a brilliant cook, always using an open fire as he had no cooker. He gave me all the freedom to come and go that I wanted at that stage in my life, without putting too many responsibilities on me.

Uncle Arthur also looked after bees as part of his job. When a swarm landed anywhere on Miss Shaw-Hellier's estate, we would fetch them. I would hold a boater hat under the swarm as it hung, say, on the bough of a tree. Arthur would then knock these bees into the hat and we would take them back to his hive. This would mean walking perhaps half a mile with all these bees! I totally hated doing this.

The beekeeping came to an abrupt end. Arthur used only a veil, no gloves or body protection, and one day he got stung in the ball of his thumb. Within minutes, his arm began to swell and his eyes became so swollen that they closed up. He sat down in the potting shed for a very long time and, thankfully, recovered. But he was spooked enough to tell Miss Shaw-Helllier that he would no longer look after her five hives.

Arthur entered the football pools each week. I gave him 2 *s.* 6 *d.* towards it. There was huge suspense once when a winning letter from Liverpool Pools arrived through the door. I had known he had won on the Saturday, because he used the same numbers to predict the football score draws each week. But he didn't say anything. He wanted to wait until the cheque arrived, I think. I had checked the numbers at Beryl's house on the Saturday night. Arthur had no clue about my having a girlfriend. He never got to know.

Arthur won a moderate amount: £2,700, split down the middle with me. I used part of my share to buy a new £700 Reliant three-wheeled car.

When I collected the car from Copes of Wolverhampton, Larry was with me and sat in the passenger seat for the journey home. Within minutes, I was stopped by the police, but there wasn't anything they could do about my possibly erratic driving. In those days, if you had passed a driving test for a motorbike of over 250cc or more (which I had) you could legally drive a three-wheeled car without L-plates. So they let me carry on! I felt like king of the road with the brightest of futures ahead.

Larry and his Friend David Ford used to go cycling. Here they are in Lynmouth Devon during the floods.

Bigun and me, near Abbotts Salford Caravan Park circa 1980s, happy as Larry. RIP

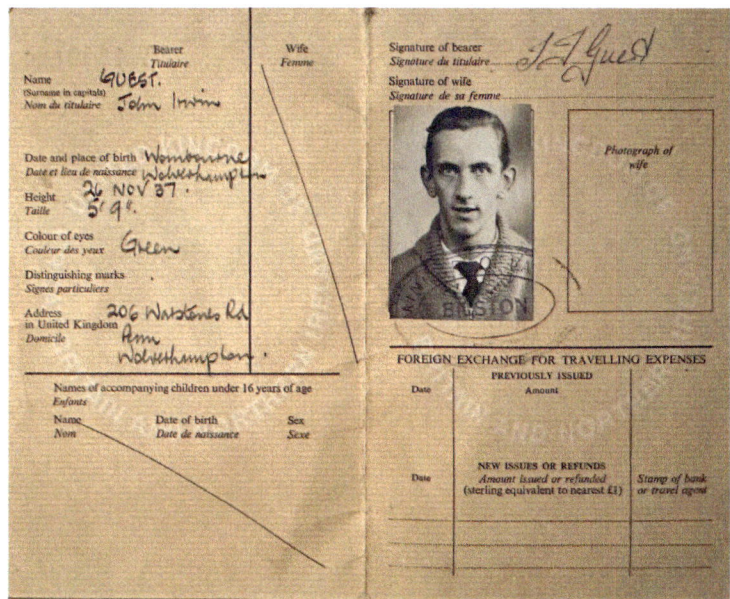

My brother the Middleun (Irwin)'s army papers. Miss you 'Herta' (nickname given by Kate). RIP. both

Two of my great work colleagues, Charles (sadly passed) and Brian, who I'm still in touch with.

6: SETTLING DOWN TO MANAGERIAL LIFE

West Bromwich Pearks was my second store as manager, and it was a larger, more prestigious posting. It was 1964 and I was just 22 years old. A Home & Colonial store traded just 60 metres along the same high street, along with a Maypole store. As I have mentioned, they were trading names within the same company and competition between them was fierce, so when I saw a PG Tips promotion in their windows, I would make sure that the district manager gave me the green light to put it in my window, too! Our main competitor in West Brom, however, was Thompson & Rose. We were part of a bustling high street that included, amongst many others, Chad's Fish and Chips and an electrical shop. This last one jogs a memory: Barbara, who worked there, would come in most mornings to buy milk and so forth. You would always know she was on the way from the screeching of brakes in cars whose drivers had taken their eyes off the road to look at her on the pavement. This was the Swinging Sixties and Barbara, who was very striking, would be wearing a low-cut top, short skirt and red high heels.

The Pearks staff at West Bromwich included Mrs Saul, who had blue-rinsed hair; Helen, nicknamed Thrifty; Dave, who delivered groceries on the store's bike; and another lad whose hair was cut into Paul McCartney's Beatles bob! I remember him one Christmas spending ages in the storeroom looking for a Mrs Peaks's Christmas pudding. At that time, customers used to ask us to 'put away' a special Christmas item – tinned salmon, Christmas cake – to collect closer to 25th December. They did it to ensure that if we ran out, they would have theirs. We'd put their name on their item before keeping it in the back room. This lad was looking for a pudding with a name label of Mrs Peaks, when that was the brand name of the pudding.

Stan Jones, the West Brom footballer, came into the store to collect a 40-pound block of Cheddar each week, which was used in his chip shop (they also sold sandwiches). He needed the cheese sliced and that took an age.

In 1965, someone tremendously important joined the store: Beryl! I will save our story for the next chapter, but suffice to say now that she was strikingly sexy and made an immediate impression on me and, I am pretty sure, a good many other young males. Guess what? She had long black hair.

Beryl's mum, Sal, also joined the store and her main job was weighing and wrapping Danish tub butter and cheese.

Sal's other job was to cut 6-pound blocks of angel, Genoa and fruit cake into either small cakes or slices. Sales of these – and also railway cake, which had jam and cream inside that looked like tracks – were unreal. Beryl's older sister, Shirley, also worked there.

Shirley left when she had her second child, Philip, who was eventually nicknamed Brush-Brush, as when Shirley brought him in he would always want to use the big shop brush to sweep up the sawdust. Larry bought him a small brush to use. Sadly, Shirley is no longer with us, and neither is her beautiful daughter, Jenny. Jenny was married to Ossy, and one year, along with Shirley's husband, Ken, we had a most memorable holiday in Agadir, Morocco.

At Pearks, the cheese was sliced with a cheese wire to each customer's request. Cheshire, Canadian, Cheddars mild to strong and Danish Blue, customers were always particular – one insisted the slice was cut to fit his cheese dish at home! The cheese wire was situated in the gap in the marble counter. The cheeses arrived in a store in wooden crates. They'd be covered for a day or so in a wet hessian sack so that 'skinning' away the outer wax cover of each cheese was easier. Even so, it was a hard task that had to be taught with care. Do it the wrong way and the cheese could split. As manager, I passed on the skills I'd learnt to my staff.

Also, in those days sugar came in 28-pound parcels. These were kept in the back store and the ones in our shop could tell a few stories if they could talk!

Our store didn't have a telephone, so we had to go to the back office at Home & Colonial if we needed to use one. One manager had a neat trick whenever he needed his glasses replaced. He would put them down on the top of the cellar steps just before the delivery guy arrived. Deliveries were busy affairs with three people sending goods down a chute into the cellar below. Typically, this manager's glasses would get cracked, and he'd put in a claim for a new pair!

The majority of people smoked in the 1960s (myself included). Customers smoked whilst they shopped, too, and there were burn marks on the wooden benches where we boned and cut bacon. If staff created a burn, typically they would use a boning knife (that had also been used to bone bacon) to scrape off the mark.

Beryl was one of the worst culprits. Horrifyingly, she also had a close shave with a boning knife. When she dropped it by accident, it became embedded in her leg. This was hugely painful and to this day she still has the scar. She also had an accident with the 'gate' – a device used to slice the end of a bacon cut. The real name for this piece of equipment was 'last-slice device'. Beryl caught her hand on its spikes.

Beryl's other store tasks were cutting up to 500 chickens a week into breast and leg portions, which would sell for two shillings and six pence each – a profit on the eight shillings. that a whole chicken would fetch. The chickens arrived frozen, but we didn't have the 'out back' fridge space to store them. The fridge, rusty and covered in greaseproof paper as it was, housed bacon, cheese and cooked meats. The thawing chickens were kept in an outside building in the backyard. Every evening, you would bring in what was needed for the next day's trade, putting it on a table at the back of the store. The following morning, when you turned on the lights, you'd hear the distinct whooshing noise of cockroaches disappearing into corners.

No one got sick.

In the window display, however, these expertly cut chicken pieces looked the bees knees when they were lined up in deep plastic trays alongside the cakes, cheeses and cooked meats. My 2-by-3-metre display always looked stunning and I became one of the top Allied Suppliers stores. I didn't know it then, but already I was being noticed by senior management. My days as a 'regular' manager were about to be paused, and for the very best of reasons.

Beryl and sister Shirley, and her Beautiful daughter Jenny on holiday in Morocco happy days. RIP Shirley and Jenny.

Carl my eldest son, our house in Redditch, and his first car, circa 1987.

7: A DOUBLE WEDDING IS ANNOUNCED!

As mentioned already, I first met Beryl when I joined the West Bromwich store. She was 15 and I was 23. I have always had a thing for girls with black hair, and Beryl had the most stunning black hair and a nice figure. Plus, she had a confidence and warmth about her.

At first, it was quite casual – Snick and I would ride over on my motorbike to the garages at the top of Basset Road (she was at number 22) and meet up with Beryl and her friend Chrissie. We had a code that if her parents were out, she would open the curtains so I would know to come inside. Beryl was part of a big, very happy family – her twin, Jacqueline, plus sisters Shirley and Pauline and brothers, George and Terry. In time, Pauline would have a son, Paul, who married Tracey and would move to Cornwall. George would marry Mildred but not leave West Brom.

There was no big proposal. It just sort of happened. Although it might not sound romantic, I think the backstory to our getting married when we did was Uncle Arthur dying.

He'd been off sick from work for a while with cancer. I had not been told what was wrong. On this evening, he was on his chair by the fireside. He coughed so much, he brought up blood, which went onto his hands.

'Get me the dish, Murphy,' he called out to me. When he started to vomit into it, I dashed out to fetch help. We didn't have a phone, of course, so I ran to the farmhouse to ring 999. By the time I had run back to our cottage, Uncle Arthur was slumped down in his chair. His lit cigarette, which he'd stood upright on the hearth of the grate, was burning steadily on. But Uncle Arthur was no longer breathing.

I remember feeling empty. In the 10 or so years that I'd lived with him, Arthur taught me so much about wildlife and rural living. He'd been just 18 – a boy really – when he'd gone off to war, and he'd returned a hard man who kept his emotions to himself.

Arthur's death affected me practically. I had to leave the tied cottage in two weeks. By this point, Mom had moved from Penn to Hastings with Tiger, and the Middle 'Un lived in Hastings, too, with his wife, Ann, and young twins, Karen and Neil. Larry still lived nearby, so I went to live with my oldest brother and his wife, June, and baby daughter, Sue. They would go on to have two more children: Sharon and Claire.

Sadly, like myself Beryl had lost her dad. I remember how heartbroken she was, as was the rest of the family.

When Beryl told me that her twin sister was pregnant and getting married to Dave in a few weeks, I said, 'Let's make it a double wedding' – much, I think, to her surprise!

We had a registry office wedding, with two brides both looking beautiful in white dresses. The date was 28th March 1968. We didn't have a honeymoon; at that time, I was very much career first. We simply didn't have the time to go away and, in fact, didn't go away for our first 'proper' holiday to Pembroke Dock, Wales until Carl was around 18 months old.

The very day that we married, we moved straight into our first home. It was over the Pearks shop in Turnberry Road, Great Barr, and accessed by iron steps at the rear of the store. The rent cost us 10 s. a month. We splashed out £25 for a lovely three-piece suite and spent around £5 per week on food.

A wedding present from Mr Gregory, my district manager at the time, was a bone china tea set, which we have to this day.

Beryl and I were truly happy in that first flat. It was relatively close to her sister Pauline's place and Pauline, her husband, Terry, and their son, Paul, were regular visitors.

For one week, Beryl managed the shop below, as a relief manager and did very well. But at that point, having children rather than building a career was uppermost on her mind.

Beryl has always been a wonderful cook and takes real pride in keeping a place neat and clean. I know she was exceptionally happy when, the following year, we moved to Hill Top, West Bromwich, and bought our first place. It was a show home and all the time we lived there, it remained just as pristine – all down to Beryl.

It cost £7,000 including fixtures, fittings, curtains and show home furniture. Allied Suppliers paid the solicitors' conveyancing fees for us. I got the mortgage from a guy I knew at West Bromwich Building Society. He shopped at Pearks and I can't remember what the sweetener was for him to give me the mortgage, but I am certain that there would have been one!

Beryl's dad had died from a heart attack two years before our marriage and as she adapted to being on her own, Beryl's mother, Sal, grew closer to us. I knew her well anyway, as she also worked at Pearks, alongside her two daughters, Beryl and Shirley.

After that first holiday to Pembroke, which was where Carl first walked, we always took Beryl's mum with us. We had some hysterical times. Once, I was driving in North Devon and the gearstick came off in my hand. Sal's face was a picture, especially when I used a block of wood as a makeshift hammer to try and put it back into place. But I still needed to call the AA to get help, and the lady at the house where I'd stopped to ask to use the phone charged me one whole shilling for making the call.

Whenever there was an opportunity, we would tease Sal silly. It was all little things; for example, when I bought some sweets that turned out to taste like pepper, I didn't tell Sal but simply said, 'Ooh, these are delicious,' and of course she asked to try one at once, and was then shocked at the true taste! Beryl wet herself laughing. But it was all in good fun and, over those early years, we had some excellent holidays together in Devon.

The lovely brides and Jackie and David. West Brom, 1968.

Beryl and me, wedding day, West Bromwich, 1968. What a journey that turned out to be. 56yrs , and counting.

Beryl and her twin sister Jackie.

Pauline, George, Shirley, Sal (Mom), Jackie, Terry and Beryl. Family photo sadly without Dad George, who had passed.

Beryl looking good in one of her many outfits. Abbots Salford Caravan Park. 1980s.

George's wife Mildred and Beryl's mom Sal, at Carl's wedding, Web Heath, Redditch. RIP Sal

Beryl's eldest brother George, with wife Mildred.

8: NOW I UNDERSTAND ...

In the 1970s, fathers were seldom at the birth of their children. So whilst Beryl laboured on at the Good Hope Hospital in Sutton Coldfield, as our firstborn was due, I kept myself busy. Work. Pacing about at home. I'd passed my driving test the year before (after only a single one-hour lesson) and now had a dark-green Ford Escort 1.6. There was no phone in our house, so I had to keep going out to a phone box to check for news from the maternity unit. When the news came on 14th August, I called my mum then Beryl's mum to tell them both that, following a forceps delivery, they had a grandson. And then I had what I would describe as amongst the most extraordinary experience of my life.

From the phone box, I'd also nipped over to Edith Street to tell Shirley. Then, my immediate tasks over, I got back into the car, and I cried. Tear upon tear. Huge shaking sobs that I can remember to this day.

I had a son! I was a dad! Yes, of course ... but what I didn't have was a dad with whom I could share the news.

My tears were for the joy of my son's arrival and for the grief of my dad's long, long-ago departure.

You may recall reading how, when I was just 10 years old, my way to deal with my dad's death was to block it out. I didn't cry. I didn't talk about it. But now, faced with the wash of emotion I felt on becoming a dad myself, I was able to connect back to what had happened all those years ago. I felt the enormity of the sadness I had carried for so many years of being the boy who grew up without a dad.

I don't know how long I cried for — as someone who never cried in those days, it seemed a very long time. Then, I grew calm once more. I wiped my face, blew my nose and drove back home.

The next day, when I was allowed on to the ward to meet 8-pound 2-ounce Carl, as we'd already decided to call our firstborn, I said nothing to Beryl. The moment had passed.

After a week, I brought Beryl and our new son home. Privately, I resolved to be the best dad I could, just as my dad had been; only, JC willing, I would be there through all of his childhood. Whereas I had had no dad to steer me through school, my first job and becoming a man, Carl would have me, always on hand with advice and support. Carl is now living with his partner, Simone, and her two daughters, Paige and Daisy.

My experience would be pretty much the same when, in 1973, our second son, Steven, was born (weight 7 pounds 12 ounces) in Clifton, at Bristol Hospital, after we'd moved to nearby Withywood the previous year. I cried private tears when I heard the news — that same mix of joy and grief. It was two full decades since my dad had died.

No Tears for Twenty Years.

No wonder my book title leapt out at me.

Today, as at last I share what I experienced and my secret promise to both boys, I am confident that Steve and Carl will feel that I have always been there for them. Some of my favourite times with the boys were on the Sundays we would spent together at the 'slough' – a wooded area close to our Redditch home. There, we'd have a fire and cook sausages and bacon etc and lark about. Beryl loved us going, too, as it meant that she could clean and prep the house to her very high standards without us all getting under her feet!

The boys would often open up to me about school, friends and so forth on our days out. Even today I feel a quiet satisfaction when, as grown men, they still choose to run past me big decisions they face: moving back to England (Steve); starting out again as a divorced dad (Carl). I'm a sounding board now, of course. Their lives and choices are their own. But I know that both my boys know that I always listen, and without judgement.

All through our marriage, I have been focused on putting in the hours and being prepared to move to wherever so that we might enjoy a good standard of living. But now I am in my 80s, I can appreciate the whole picture.

To show strong emotion isn't to be weak, and neither is sharing any tears that happen as a result. Dad has been gone nearly 70 years now and I still grieve for all that I missed out on when this amazing, kind and mild-mannered man was taken from me. Today, I always shed a tear talking about him and all my family who have passed on.

Eldest son Carl, 1972, Withywood, Bristol, company flat. Memories.

Carl on the canal, Redditch.

Beryl with Carl, pregnant with Steve, Chew Magna near Bristol. 1972

Carl outside of our company flat in Withywood Bristol 1972, dog is not real, but used to Bark.

Steven, Redditch. 1983 ?

Carl Redditch 1983 ?

The Boys, Bristol, Flat in Withywood, i was the Manager of, Liptons Thornbury, at this time.

9: PROMOTION AND PROMOTIONS!

I was living with Beryl and Baby Carl at Hill Top, West Bromwich, and still manager at West Brom, in 1971 when decimalisation began. Explaining why everything was 'rounded up' to the new halfpennies, which were worth so much more than the previous halfpennies, was no fun. 'How much is that in old money?' customers would ask (and for years afterwards, they would still ask!). Five pence was the old sixpence; 10 pence was the old shilling, and 50 pence the old 10 bob. Challenging times.

I must have handled it OK, though, because before the year was out I was promoted to assistant district manager level. It meant moving to and overseeing stores in the Bristol area. I was so ambitious that I didn't even consult Beryl before I said yes to the job offer, even though I knew it would mean moving the family home.

We put our house up for £11,000 and sold it within a fortnight. I agreed to move into another company flat, this time in Withywood, Bristol.

It was a terrible mistake. Downgrading from our own lovely house and garden to a rented company flat brought no joy for Beryl. The flat was over a Lipton store, so, again, steps for Beryl, now juggling a toddler and a buggy. But at that time, my eye was on the prize. A bigger job, a larger salary, a career going in the up, up direction.

Cavenham Foods acquired Allied Suppliers just after I had made the Bristol move. At just £92 million, it was a cheeky takeover, engineered by Jimmy Goldsmith. When he revalued all the buildings previously owned by Allied, they turned out to be worth more than he'd paid for the company. So in a way, he got the good name of the stores and their stock for free.

My new area manager, Don O'Leary, lived in Bristol. Other new colleagues were Mr Glanville, Andy Bowen, Peter Booth and Mr Norris, the Withywood store manager, who eventually moved to the Lipton store in Gibraltar where he stayed until retirement.

One day, Irwin visited us at home and made a shocking discovery. The rented flat had mice! Chewed newspaper under a sofa cushion was the giveaway. To our horror, Beryl and I realised that what we had thought was a spider crawling over our faces at night was in all probability a mouse.

The warehouse below had mice, most warehouses did. But where had it – hopefully 'it' rather than 'they' – got into our flat? That very evening, whilst I was on the toilet, I discovered the way in had been via the space where the toilet bend joined the floor. A mouse conveniently proved it for me by running from the toilet into the living room and up the curtain.

Beryl, who was and is afraid of mice, went into the bedroom with Carl and Steven and closed the door firmly. I took a shoe and, holding it against the curtain, smacked the moving mouse. Job done. I then sealed the hole around the toilet pipe and we never saw any mice again.

It was 1974, and when regional director Alex Atkinson summoned me to the Worcester head office, I had an inkling it was for promotion to district manager. As I drove to Worcester in my Escort 1.6 company car, I reflected on how happy I was to now be the father of two brilliant boys. There had been a special moment after Steve's birth when, as Carl and I were waiting to see Beryl and Steve in hospital, I watched Carl playing with a tin of toy monkeys I had bought and thought how my firstborn was growing up fast. Life was good and I wondered, amongst other things, what larger car I might soon be driving...

In Alex's office, his first questions threw me. They were about my mileage use, and he said I had been overestimating it and showed me my weekly logs. I had never done this, but pointed out that a fruit and veg trainer had used my car as well, for a legitimate business journey, due to a fault with his own vehicle.

'Guest,' he said flatly, 'I'm busting you.'

I broke down.

Thank goodness 'busting you' meant that he was stripping me from my position, not from the company itself.

'From next week, you will be going into our Clifton store as manager,' he continued. I was allowed to keep the Escort – goodness knows why. I have seldom felt so low in my adult life as when I drove home to break the news to Beryl. To my surprise, she wasn't surprised; she simply and calmly accepted what I'd been told and continued being the wonderful mum she has always been, managing very well indeed on my new, reduced salary.

Lipton Clifton was one of the stores I had visited as assistant district manager. I took it on the chin that now district manager Andy Bowen was visiting me as manager at the same store I'd had senior responsibility for previously.

Happily, Andy was as nice a man as you might meet, but he wasn't always the most prudent. Once, he hired a man who'd told him he was a lay preacher. But it turned out this chap was no saint – one week he didn't bank the takings and ran off with the money, never to be seen again! Andy came from South Wales and liked a joke. One day, I'd been listening to Radio 4 in the car and a caller had posed the question, 'How is it we can teach parrots to talk, yet the nearest creature to man is a monkey and we can't teach them speech?' There was no real answer on the radio programme, so I asked Andy during a tea break.

'Monkeys can talk,' he quipped back, 'but they make-believe they can't in case we ask them to do some work.' So funny at the time.

Clifton Lipton was a small store, mostly shopped in by university students. It had a turnover of just £20,000 a week. From the start, I vowed to change that. I wrote on my weekly 'digest sheet' that I would increase the turnover by £5,000 in six months. In fact, it took me less than six months. I remember writing on the very next digest sheet 'I am better than I thought I was.'

Whilst I was supposedly managing Clifton full-time, my old boss Don O'Leary would get me to help him in his stores as well. It meant I put in long hours, but at least I had Sundays free for the family. Supermarkets being open on Sundays wouldn't come in until 1994, and this was the 1970s. We'd take lovely walks at Chew Reservoir, taking turns to push the pram. We felt settled once more.

Then, quite out of the blue, Don said Alex had told him that he wanted me to open the Thornbury Discount Lipton store.

I said, 'No, I want to stay where I am.'

Alex went ballistic. I was summoned – again – to Worcester HQ where his rage continued.

'Who do you think you are, turning down managing what will be our flagship store?' he blasted.

I emerged from Alex's office having accepted the position of manager at Thornbury. I had no choice.

Finally, I got the better car I'd had my eye on before my last, disastrous meeting with Alex. Don was changing his company Cortina and it was agreed I could buy it from Cavenham for £500. In the months it took to finalise our house move, I'd commute from Bristol to Thornbury. My drive was on the flight path of Concorde, the supersonic jet that was being built and tested out in nearby Filton. The noise and shadow it cast as it whizzed past was breathtaking.

Lipton Thornbury was a fantastic store, principally due to its staff. I recall the butchery manager, Mervin Law, who came from Lipton Gibraltar and whom I am still in contact with 50 odd years later, and Mrs Marshall who ran the warehouse and oversaw pricing. Every item back then needed to be priced with a label stuck onto it with a Pitney Bowes gun, and there were thousands of these to do each week. There was Ann on the deli who, with her husband Les, would go on to be a good friend for many years, and Alison who did the bookwork. Alison's father helped me each evening to clean the shop floor with mops and buckets. We both got £20 per week, cash, for doing that back-breaking task. No floor-cleaning machines there.

Other staff members included Carol on wines and spirits. Carol was so naturally good-looking that I suggested she should enter the local beauty competition. When she said that she couldn't afford the entrance fee, I said that I would pay – on the condition that she split her winnings! She returned from the contest the triumphant winner.

'Let me give you half of my prize money,' she said. Naturally, I told her to keep it all.

In 1974, whilst I was at Thornbury, there was a national sugar shortage. Customers were allowed to buy one bag per day. Once, I was called to the checkouts urgently. A customer was using an umbrella to hit a lad on the checkout who said she couldn't buy two bags. The customer isn't always right in situations like this.

A girl on the non-food department had a crush on the non-food area manager. We'd know he had a visit booked because she always did her hair and make-up. Store gossip was that this area manager was also familiar with this girl's home, and in particular the back garden. Word was that her neighbours saw him jump the fence onto the street when the girl's partner suddenly returned home!

One distressing incident involving Carl happened around this time. I'd picked up a Chinese takeaway and, eating it at home, I tucked into chow mein and fried rice. Carl was still up and I gave him a small amount of fried rice. The following evening when I got home from work, Beryl was hugging Carl.

'He's not right,' she told me. He had diarrhoea and a high temperature. At Southmead Hospital, the registrar said that Carl was so unwell, he would need to be admitted. Beryl and I were in bits. I got word to district manager Peter Booth that I wouldn't be in work the next day. Thankfully, by the time we saw Carl the following morning, he had begun to recover. The consultant, Mr McWade, told us it was salmonella poisoning, and, after the results of stool samples from the rest of us came back, the Chinese food was found to be the culprit. Whilst I didn't become physically unwell, the fact that these tests showed that I was carrying salmonella too meant I had to stay off work, I think for between four and five weeks. It was the first time I had ever taken sick leave from work. I'm not sure what the public health department did about the Chinese restaurant, but we never returned.

I'd first met Peter Booth during apprenticeship training days in London. He told me that in the second year of trading, my store would change from 'discount' to the next level up the pricing ladder. I thought of all the hard work that would mean. Remember, everything was hand-priced. When the price of products went down, you could simply stick on a red label with the new price. When it went up, you had to peel away the old sticker then reprice. At the time, our store traded with 'standard discount'. (If there had been big competition in the same neighbourhood, a store might be rated 'markdown' instead.) To ensure we managed to sell everything at the correct price on the day the store stopped being a discount branch, I decided that whenever we got new price lists, we would sell existing new stock at that standard price. That way not everything had to change overnight. The store went from strength to strength and remained a top store at its new level.

Settling in as the Thornbury manager also gave me the chance to put right the mistake of the rented flat in Withywood.

Whilst Thornbury was doing great under great colleagues, other stores were floundering. Results at the Cheltenham store were poor. 'When are you going to take Cheltenham?' Don O'Leary and Peter Booth would regularly ask. I kept saying no. I didn't want to leave my Lipton colleagues who had made Thornbury great. Then, one Friday, I decided to play Devil's advocate.

'If I were to say yes, what sort of a pay rise and guaranteed bonus would you be offering?' I ventured. 'Plus, I would never take the job without being given a deposit for my next home.'

On Monday morning Don and Peter were at my Thornbury store early doors.

'Alex Atkinson has agreed to your requests. The deal is that you move as soon as possible.'

That Sunday, Beryl and I went house-hunting and put a £50 holding deposit on an £8,500 property at the new Heron Park development in Gloucester. The full deposit of £850 for 22 Curlew Road, along with its carpets, curtains and solicitors' fees, was paid for by Cavenham Foods and we took a mortgage with Lloyds for the rest. I had a better job. Beryl was happy once more in our owned home. A win-win situation.

Our new home was end terrace with a small front and back garden and a garage in a block. We had lovely neighbours in Shirley and John (who had Margo and Raymond and came from the USA), Ingrid and Pete, and Sue and Pete, who was in the merchant navy. Carl, now four years old, soon started school at Coney Hill Infants. He began mornings only, as they sometimes do, and there was a blip on his first full day when Carl took himself out of school at midday and walked home. He arrived safely, but Beryl was not happy that the school had not noticed!

Another hiccup was when the junior school on Heron Park said they were too full to admit Carl. I made an appointment with Sally Oppenheim-Barnes then Conservative MP for Gloucester, (now Baroness Oppenheim-Barnes)and a place for my son was swiftly found.

A brilliant holiday in that time was when we went to Rimini, Italy, in 1978. The boys were looked after on the beach by an old couple; we hardly saw them, and they had such fun!

Curlew Road was a happy time for us over the years that we lived there. It was quiet enough to play shuttlecock in the street. There was also a brook nearby, where Carl, Steve and I would successfully fish for eels at night using a worm on a small hook and a light. Sal often stayed and Beryl's youngest brother, Terry, was a frequent visitor too. He was around 12 at that time and would run round and round the nearby football pitch saying he was 'in training'. For what, I never discovered. Terry now lives in Cornwall with his partner, Sandra.

One day, I was painting the outside of the house when I became distracted by the kids out using their skateboards. I had to have a go!

Aged 32, and fit enough to do 32 pull-ups a day using the top of garden swings as my bar, I reckoned I could give these youngsters a run for their money. The kids had put two empty milk crates along the sloping path by the side of our house and were skateboarding between them, picking up great downhill speeds.

I jumped on, hurtling down as fast as a rabbit on a promise, only to come off the board and fall onto the path.

Everybody, including Beryl, laughed and laughed – until they saw what pain I was in. It was my shoulder. I crawled into the car, taking young Terry with me. With Terry in charge of the gearstick and changing it on my command, I drove to Royal Gloucester Hospital A & E. Nothing was broken, thankfully, but my shoulder stayed in a sling for a while.

With our own home, we were able to host great parties for our neighbours and friends. Drink was involved and these were very lively occasions, especially at Christmas and New Year, and included fun games, like postman's knock where you got to go for a snog with the person whose number was guessed. Repeatedly, I ended up with Ingrid and Beryl with Pete. I soon cottoned on to how it was that this happened: Ingrid and Pete were signalling to each other. All good fun.

One year, we had two houses to choose from, since Shirley and John had also given us the keys to their place next door as they were going away. That led to a tremendous game of hide-and-seek. It was pitch-dark and in the pandemonium, our neighbours' upstairs front curtains came off the rail and young Terry, who had been hiding under the bed next door, got covered in fluff and dust because Shirley wasn't as good a housekeeper as Beryl! On a different year, when her husband was away with the merchant navy, Sue was dancing on the table wearing only a pair of knickers . . . on her head.

John next door was the manager of the Fyffes bananas depot and drove a Hillman car. My assistant district manager status qualified me for a company car, so I sold my Cortina to John. He then tried to sell his Hillman. It was probably worth £800, and John received offers at this amount, but Shirley insisted they accept nothing lower than £1,000. Result? No takers. Over a long period of non-use and kids playing on it, the car looked fit only for the scrapyard. I went with John when, finally, he dropped it off there. As the battery was still OK, they gave him £5. When I could stop laughing, I drove us both to the pub where John then spent the full fiver!

At work, I turned Lipton Cheltenham from being 2 per cent below budget to a 3 per cent profit. My secret? As ever, it was happy colleagues.

In 1977, I moved on from Cheltenham to work directly for the head of merchandising, George Wood, along with a colleague, Haydn Ebbs. Our role was to focus on stores that George identified as having potential to improve. We were part of a big region now with plenty of stores with potential. We went together to pick up new company cars, both Ford Escorts.

'You're the one with kids,' said Haydn, 'so I'll take the two-door and you have the four-door.' That very day we pulled up by a steep embankment between store visits to talk about something. When we got back into our cars, Haydn had forgotten to close his passenger door and it caught the embankment. Ouch! I think he reported the resultant damage.

My new merchandising role saw Haydn and myself introduce change at stores trading under the Moores name. These belonged to a company that Cavenham Foods had bought out. They were to be re-branded as Lipton. All good, except customers would no longer receive the Green Shield Stamps they had been given at Moores. This hugely popular bonus scheme, which ran at petrol stations and many high-street stores, enabled customers to build up big collections of stamps that they could exchange for kettles, saucepans, even camping gear and so forth. As well as managing customer expectations (i.e. no more stamps), we had to handle resentment from some staff in the stores that had been taken over, including the Caldicot store. This was located just past the Severn Bridge taking you into Wales. Haydn and I worked hard to create a different look and to get staff on board. By Saturday evening, all looked great and ready for the Monday switch.

Job done, we were at another store on Monday when a call came in from our boss, George Wood, asking if we had completed the refurb, as John Feldon, the regional director, had just called in there. There were no posters up and the store was looking drab. Had store management taken them down in protest? I never got to the bottom of it, but the manager of that store didn't stay with Lipton for long.

In 1976, I was promoted to district manager, South Wales, working under Area Manager Jimmy Skidmore and Regional Director Des James. A part of my role was trying to convince ex-Moores colleagues that the future was Lipton. After another district manager in Leicester suffered serious injuries in a road accident, I became district manager for that area too, which, perhaps bizarrely, also included stores around Oxford. My boss insisted I visit the injured district manager's home and ask his wife for his briefcase with all his district's paperwork. She was not pleased to see me and threw the briefcase at me. She obviously didn't like Jimmy.

During my district manager years, I covered tremendous mileage. Stores I was responsible for included those in Tonypandy, Aberdare and Treorchy amongst many others. In one store near the Rhigos Mountains, locals insisted a ghost prowled the place.

'Have you seen it?' I was asked.

Quick as a flash I answered, 'It won't show up when I'm around, because it knows I might ask it to do some work.'

Visiting the Merthyr Tydfil store meant passing the graveyard where the 144 casualties of the 1996 Aberfan disaster lay buried. When I thought on how some 116 were children, I had to stop the car and weep.

I could weep now when something profound or greatly sad happened and have continued to be able to do so ever since that 'unlocking' of my emotions when Carl and Steve were born. That day, in Merthyr Tydfil, I felt how precious life is.

And also how what we have and experience each day becomes our memories tomorrow.

Stepping into Treorchy Moores, which I also covered, was like stepping back in time. Flagstone floors. Fruit and veg kept in the bags they had been delivered to the store in. Manual platform weighing scales, plus a single lightbulb suspended from the ceilings. It reminded me of when I had begun in retailing in the 1950s. The staff were wonderful. I remember the manager especially, a lovely lady. She took me to a clothing outlet called Polycoffs that made suits for Marks & Spencer and I bought one for just £10.

Eventually, I had to deliver the devastating news that Treorchy was to be closed. I will never forget the distress of three of the women in particular who had each worked there for many years. I was glad that, by the time we finally closed the doors, clever closing stock figures by me meant that these women would not have to buy sugar, tea or coffee for a very long time. I found a way to allocate these items away from the stock results, yet still come in with a surplus stock result. I even delivered the 'swag' to these ladies' homes. It felt the least I could do.

At a district managers meeting in Worcester, a new chap with the company, Brian Springthorpe, asked a question that caused a stir: 'Have any of you stolen anything from the company?'

Silence.

'So no one has taken a pen from a store?'

You could have heard a pin drop in that meeting.

That same day, driving back, I pranged into the back of another district manager when he pulled up sharply. My fault entirely. Thankfully, there was only minimal damage to each car.

On 27th December 1976, I set off at 6 a.m. to visit a store in Wales. I was going to take my nephew Terry with me, who had been with us for Christmas, but at the last minute, he decided he would rather stay in his cosy bed! It was still dark, but the roads around Gloucester were fine. However, conditions had deteriorated by the time I reached the Forest of Dean. Suddenly, I lost control on black ice. I had been travelling at around 40 miles per hour. I wasn't wearing a seatbelt and there were no in-car airbags back then.

As my car spun towards the trees on the central reservation, I put one arm in front of my face and braced myself.

Next thing, someone was getting me out of the car and saying, 'Let's get this man back to the side of the road.'

I wasn't the only driver to crash. In all, five cars had skidded on the ice. One driver was fatally injured when his Mini overturned on the embankment.

My car was wrapped around the tree and I find it incredible that I sustained only a cut on my head from hitting the interior mirror and a painful knee. Had young Terry come with me, judging by the way the tree had wedged into the passenger side of the car, I shudder to think what might have happened to him.

A police officer who arrived soon at the scene suggested hospital, but I declined. He also hinted that I might be prosecuted for driving too fast in appalling conditions.

I exited the situation quickly to ring Jimmy Skidmore. I hadn't expected, and didn't receive, any sympathy.

'Get the train to Wales then,' was his blunt reply.

Typical Jimmy.

It was one day soon afterwards that a big change came my way. I was on a store visit to Oxford when I received a phone call from George Wood setting up a meeting with Bill Head, a director, and myself at an M5 service station. All very cloak-and-dagger!

At this meeting, I was told that Liptons would soon be a thing of the past and Presto was the future.

'Clive, you need to be part of this future,' I was told before being offered a salary increase that would have tempted anyone.

The offer was to take the general manager's role in the Cheltenham store, the same Lipton that I had been manager of before becoming a district manager. It would be the company's largest Lipton conversion and was a true flagship store. The devious bit was that there was, of course, a current general manager who was expecting to take to the helm himself once it became a Presto.

The company let this guy work during the conversion, then told him about me. He was not happy and asked for all the overtime hours he had put in without charge (as managers typically have to do) to be paid right away. The company had to agree. In his shoes, I would have done the same.

My time running Presto Cheltenham from 1978 until 1980 holds many memories. My deputy, Doug Fleming, was great.

His biggest asset was organising and planning; his biggest downfall was poor eyesight, even with glasses. Once, he pushed a stock trolley with cases of jam on board onto a lift platform – only the platform wasn't there, so he pushed the trolley into an open drop of 6 feet. What a sticky mess! I learnt to keep him away from replenishing anything breakable. Once, he mistook George Wood for the postman. Another time, his wife rang the store at 9 p.m. because he wasn't home, yet he had left the store at 5 p.m. It turned out that poor-sighted Doug had got onto the wrong bus, and it took hours to double back then get the right one. When I arranged for a report on his eyesight, it came back saying there were no medical issues but he shouldn't drive. I took that to mean trolleys with breakable goods, too!

The day that our warehouse manager, Gerald, moved big boss Bill Head's car didn't go too well either. Bill had blocked in a delivery lorry, so Gerald had to move the car, but unfortunately he backed into a wall.

Now and again, junior staff got out of hand. Once, a couple of lads roped together the ankles of a young man who had been boasting about being very wealthy and coming into work in a flash car. They hung him up with an S-hook in the chiller along with the sides of bacon. Thankfully, I heard about it within the hour and stopped this.

As we lived relatively locally to the store, one of the lads, Eddie O'Byrne, was up for babysitting for us at our Gloucester house on the rare occasions we went out. He was a lovely young man – mad on the Osmonds pop group, and I think he may also have become a Mormon.

My Presto Cheltenham store did extremely well. The company was aggressive in its pricing and soon had very experienced people in charge, namelynamely director, Tom Gartland (previously Presto North), and David Hazel (previously Presto Halesowen). Tom and I had a few heated moments, but David and I were calmer together – I had known him since the 1960s, after all. We ran a tight ship at Cheltenham with regards to food waste. For example, I remember that excess leaves that fell away from the cabbages ended up finely chopped up and on sale in the deli's coleslaw!

One ongoing initiative at Presto was each store's Carnival Fund. At this time, general managers did their buying for their store direct from suppliers – United Biscuits and the like would send their reps into each store to secure orders.

The Carnival Fund was a way that reps could do their deals: if we agreed to actively promote a product with, for example, premium shelf space, they would write a cheque out to the Carnival Fund. All monies collected would be used on the anniversary of the store opening. *A lot* of money was generated this way. Some years it could be as much as £8,000. The reps also gave gifts directly to store managers – I know of one who had his lounge furnished by (I think) United Biscuits!

I got in on the action. Of course I did! It was tax-free and, as I mentioned at the beginning of the book, I never paid for a cigarette or any alcohol during these years, nor did I have to shell out for kids' bikes, TVs, washing machines and so forth. Other reps gave M & S vouchers, which I presented to Beryl each Christmas.

A further nice little earner was when I caught a bread delivery driver swapping date tags on his bread (effectively passing off staler bread as fresh). If I reported him, he'd lose his job and we'd also, I felt, lose the contract with that company. He gave me Jackson the Tailor vouchers, swore never to do it again, and we both said nothing.

Doug organised a Sunday football match between staff at Presto Kingswood, Bristol and ourselves. We filled a coach for the drive to Bristol. I even played in the first half!

The next day, back at Presto, I was parking my car when Eddie O'Byrne called out to me. It was 6 a.m. and I'd come in early to open up for the cleaners. Eddie had left Presto by now and was working on the council dustbin carts, so he was out early, too. 'Sir,' he shouted out. 'A red car has passed the store four times and driving is a guy that was with us at the football.'

I thought no more of it and went into the store. I let the cleaners in, at the same time picking a brown envelope up from the mat inside. I thought no more about that, either, and chucked it onto the desk for later.

After a word with the cleaners, I returned to my office.

The envelope simply said 'Manager'. Inside was a message composed from cut-out letters from a newspaper. It read:

> *Just after you left home this morning, we broke into your home and we have got your wife Beryl and children Carl and Steven. If you ever want to see them again, take the money from the safe and put it on the passenger seat of your car. Do not ring the police as we are monitoring the phone every second.*

I froze.

The terror that filled me, you just cannot imagine. Whilst it might have seemed that I lived for my work, it was my family I loved. They meant – and mean – everything to me.

I knew I would pay anything to keep them safe. But I knew also that I couldn't get the money. The safe needed a key *and* combination. I held the key; the cashier, Joan, had the combination.

In pure panic, I phoned Beryl. Her hello sounded as it always did.

'Is anyone else in the house?'

'No. Just me and the kids.'

I told her to lock the door and answer to no one.

Next I phoned the police. They arrived very swiftly, and then just as quickly went to Curlew Road, where they searched the place top to bottom. Next, Beryl, myself and the children went to Cheltenham Police Station to give a statement.

Initially, I believe the police wrongly suspected Eddie. But I knew it wouldn't have been him and, of course, it was not. There was another suspect, but no one was ever charged. It would appear that the extent of the malice was to send me that ransom demand rather than carry anything out. But it was a horrific experience for both myself and Beryl.

Italy, 1978, pulled there Beryl, Carl n Steve look a bit concerned ,like the dress,

Ossy, Phil, (Jens brother) Carl, Steve, and Jenny in a Burba village Morroco, R.I.P. Jenny. great holiday.

Our neighbors, in Curlew Rd, Gloucester, Margo and Raymond, went back to the USA, with their mom , Shirley, great kids.

Steve Carl, and their friends at Curlew Rd, Gloucester, Water damage from Evesham floods. in the picture.

On the road to Marrakesh, the most Vibrant , place i ever encountered fab holiday,

Holiday in Morroco, with Shirley, Ken, Jenny, (RIP) and Ossy, great time, Wheres Phil ? buying shoes,? lol

Penbroke Dock, Carl took his first steps this day, 2 little girls used to take him out in his pushchair, everyday, 1971.

10: ONE IN A MILLION – TIMES FOUR!

In late 1979, Tom Gartland and the area manager visited Presto Cheltenham and asked me to go out to lunch. It was the most delicious cooked ham, new potatoes and peas ever. I had no idea what the purpose was.

After lunch we travelled towards Birmingham. We pulled up outside a cinema in Sheldon. 'This is going to become our next Presto,' I was told, 'and we would like you to launch it.'

I did not hesitate. On Sunday, Beryl, the kids and I went house-hunting. Again, we went for a new build. It was on a development called Greensleeves in Redditch. Number 31 Campden Close was a three-bedroom detached house, and again, the company footed the bill for solicitor costs, carpets and curtains. Our previous house sold easily. A Chinese couple bought it and, so I was told, only a week later they accidentally set fire to the kitchen.

Both Carl and Steve began at Harry Taylor Junior School, Redditch, and, again, we found ourselves with great new neighbours. This time, there were many children too, and the cul-de-sac was quiet enough for them to play out in the street. The boys' friends included Karen , Yvonne, Donna, Steve, Jason and Dave.

I needed four weeks off work when I developed a hernia. I was in Smallwood Hospital for seven days. Everyone else was elderly. One dinner time, just as tomato soup had been served, a fly appeared. It buzzed about before settling on one chap's bowl. As he attempted to hit it with a spoon, the bowl broke and soup went everywhere. I laughed that hard I thought my stitches would split.

By this point, Beryl had begun working at Kwik Save, as had our friend Pat. We were such good friends that we'd holiday together with Pat and Trevor's son, Dean, who was around Carl's age. I'd acquired some quality tents (thanks to a food rep, of course) and before our main holiday at Brean Sands, Trevor and I took the boys on a three-night test run to a campsite near Worcester.

At the time, Trevor and I were both big whisky drinkers and so, tents up, we were enjoying a few drams when a soft-top car parked next to us. Out hopped two girls and, being knights in shining armour, we put up their tents. They then drove off and, strangely, didn't come back to their tents until three days later. The camping test was, however, a great success — so next up was Brean. We had to wait in our cars for several hours before the rain cleared enough for us to begin to put up our tents. Trevor — who's known a little for his short temper — could then be heard from inside their canvas: 'Pat! Hold it steady for f***'s sake. Hold the f***ing thing straight!'

From inside our easy-to-put together tent, Beryl was close to wetting herself with laughter.

A much-talked-about incident with Trevor (who has now sadly passed away) was in the early Safeway days. Safeway had sayings with regard to store systems, and when our area manager had a store managers meeting, there would be a guest speaker. Once it was a Safeway produce trainer.

Trevor and I were sitting next to each other and when the speaker said, 'The first thing I want to talk about is the five o'clock programme,' Trevor looked at me and smiled.

Immediately the speaker said, 'Did I say something funny?'

Trevor stood up and replied, 'No you f***ing didn't, as if you had you would have heard me f***ing laugh.'

The guy picked up his briefcase and said to Trigger, our nickname for District Manager Roy Walters, 'Can't you control your managers?' and left!

Now I come to the story I promised about Arthur's brother Jack. I had kept in touch with Jack ever since Arthur died. His wife, Annie, had died and I'd visit him every few weeks, taking with me a bottle of whisky. Now and again, I'd bring him back to Redditch for one of Beryl's Sunday dinners (never to be bettered by anyone!). One day, a lady rang from Seisdon, where Jack lived. She told me he had fallen down the stairs and died. My brothers and I arranged his funeral and everyone said that I was bound to inherit everything. I was optimistic, too. On the day of the will reading, held at Jack's house, Middle 'Un nudged me in the ribs as the solicitor read out . . . that Jack had left everything to his next-door neighbour. It came out that he had been knocking her off for years. I took my two shotguns away that day (they had been at Jack's house, from way back when I was with Arthur). Later, I had a letter from the solicitor asking me to return them. I told them they were mine and the firearms certificate proved this, and to get lost!

Presto Sheldon opened in 1980. The beauty of opening a new store was that you helped to choose the staff. I took on a mix of people I'd worked with before and new faces. I would say, 'Give me a hundred per cent and I will give you back one hundred and twenty per cent. But give me less, and you will get nothing.'

Just before we opened, we put on a meal for all department managers. It was served on a table on the shop floor and put together by merchandiser Dave Wong. Dave was also an interpreter at courts in London when they needed Chinese speakers, and his attention to detail was unbelievable. He wrote out, in immaculate Chinese symbols of course, every menu item for the feast, which was then fulfilled by a local restaurant. The meal was something to behold, as was the menu for the table – in both English and Chinese – which I have as a memento to this day.

My people manager at Presto Sheldon was Jean Marshall. One day, when the area manager visited, I'd done something or other that was worthy of celebration. He got a bottle of champagne from the shop floor and popped it in my office. The cork flew up to hit the fluorescent lights – which shattered all over Jean. 'That's put the cat amongst the spokes,' he said. Just those words. 'Spokes' when it should have been 'pigeons'. The area manager was like that – always getting popular phrases muddled up.

Janet in the Sheldon cash office went on to marry Ken Firkins, one of the managers. Ken's claim to fame was that he used to chauffeur top showman, Larry 'Shut-That-Door' Grayson. Other notable colleagues were Richard Holmes, my deputy; his brother Brian, who was a stocktaker; Phil Court, the produce manager; Little Stan from the warehouse, who once temporarily locked both my sons into one of the received goods cages and affixed the sign 'Do not feed the monkeys'; and Carol, who had a tripping accident by the back-up freezer. I can see her now, one foot forwards, one spread backwards, waiting for the ambulance crew. I am and am not ashamed to say that, as the paramedics carried her out, I asked her for her orders sheet for the next day's trading!

A memory about Phil Court. He and the area manager had a good relationship – Phil was produce manager at that time. One evening, a lad looking after the outside trolleys brought in a 56-pound sack of potatoes he'd found in the car park. I asked Phil about them. He told me he'd put them by the area manager's back wheel, but he had obviously forgotten to put them in his boot!

People described me as firm but fair and I remain happy with that. For the next four years I was at the helm – yet again – of a top store. Net profits were typically 12–13 per cent and at one point reached 14 per cent. How proud I felt when Tom Gartland said that, in all his years, he had never seen a 14 per cent profit-and-loss sheet.

Presto promotions were second to none. Once, we had a raffle to win a new Austin Mini Metro. The car itself stood in the store and Julie (the daughter of Pam in produce) wore a gold sash as she stood next to it all day to draw customers' attention to what they might win.

One night, in an attempted theft, a car rammed the front doors of the store. Police conducted a full search, with dogs, in case any of the thieves were still inside. They weren't but one of the officers got trapped by a polystyrene panel and was jumped at by the dog. I can hear him now: 'Get that f***ing dog off my leg!'

We used the electronic branch ordering system (EBOS) to control stock levels. It had just been rolled out and there were glitches, principally when the unit beeped to indicate a low battery. Then, it might misread what was needed – once, we ended up with 400 cases of marrowfat peas! I rang to get this cancelled, but had no joy. I learnt that you had to do what EBOS had decided. My stock and systems guy was Nick Booth, and believe me you could ask him to order any particular product and he would remember the product number.

Another massive Presto promotion was a full page of money-off coupons that would be printed in national newspapers. Customers could cut out what they wanted for an instant discount from a particular product they bought. But a lot of jiggery-pokery happened as well. Rumour had it (I would say fact) that one store used a guillotine in the staffroom to cut coupons out of newspapers (which, of course, were sold in-store). These coupons would then be put through the tills when no products were actually bought. But the money would be pocketed.

There was one stocktaker who called at the store. I said to him casually one day, 'I bet you are taking all the coupons to X gate–,' and I named a store which put them through the till.

'How do you know that?' he asked.

'I didn't. But I do now as you have just told me.'

My store's receptionist, Sue, was a bubbly girl, so I knew something had happened when one busy Friday she very quietly told me she had just taken a short phone call.

The caller had said, 'There is a bomb in the store,' and hung up.

This wasn't that many years after the dreadful Birmingham pub bombings, when 21 people were killed, and I knew I had to act at once. I knew also that many, many places received bomb threats that were hoaxes.

I called the police. I was told that if we closed the store, we would be sure to get many more calls like this. If we did nothing, chances were we wouldn't get another call.

Decision time.

I got the department heads together and told them to have a good look around the store, particularly under fixtures. I told them only that someone had lost a handbag with a high value of cash inside.

Nothing was found and Sue never breathed a word.

It was a few weeks later that I told my deputy, Dave Collins, the truth.

He was not amused. I don't think I would have been, either, if the shoe had been on the other foot.

Or – perish the thought – it had not been a hoax.

Helen Green looked after wines and spirits. Her son worked for Austin Works in Solihull and as such was entitled to a hefty discount on new cars. Through him, I took possession of a Vanden Plas Austin Metro for a cracking price.

Thanks, Helen! Some 43 years on, I live on the same retirement park as Helen, who is now in her 90s.

Martin Downes and Mick McCarthy were two more real characters. Mick used to walk with a folded umbrella. Martin was just a truly fun guy whom I worked with again in later years.

Another decade, another takeover . . . now we were Argyll, whose CEO, Alistair Grant, would in time get a knighthood for services to retail and charity. By 1982, Argyll was the UK's fourth biggest retailer. In 1983, Alistair Grant visited the Sheldon store.

'Why,' he asked me, 'do you choose large volume (but low cost) items like toilet rolls and cornflakes for the front of the store?'

'Easy, Mr Grant. The customers then choose to use trolleys not baskets!'

I could tell my answer impressed both him and my direct boss, Tom Gartland, who was with Sir Alistair.

However, a later answer of mine didn't go down well at all.

'So who will win the FA cup tomorrow, Clive?'

It was Man United versus Brighton.

'Brighton,' I replied. How was I supposed to know that he had a supporters box at Old Trafford!

I knew now, of course, and when I saw him again, I would draw on that knowledge.

It was around this time that I successfully overcame my fear of the dentist. I'd been fearful of the dentist who visited my junior school, so kept away in adulthood until tooth pain meant I finally had to do something about it – I needed eight extractions and six fillings. I had them done on the Friday; I was back to work on the Monday.

Throughout my time at Sheldon Presto, the managers' perks kept on coming. These really were my years of plenty. I recall Burton's Biscuits bought my suits; another company provided a top-of-the-range microwave and one Christmas I was able to pass on to Beryl £2,000 in M & S vouchers, all courtesy of the reps.

I would see around 20 sales reps over a month – all the big names from Birds Eye, Gillette, Ross, Findus, RHM Beechams and so forth. Special deals would be done and our profit margins set, plus there would be a cheque for the Carnival Fund as often as not. This went so well that one year I put a sign on the customer service desk in January, where the reps would sign in (but which customers of course couldn't see). It read: 'This store enjoyed a very buoyant trade in 1980, and if you would like to be part of this year's activity, a cheque for £20 for the Carnival Fund would be very welcome.'

KP crisps gave Olympic racing bikes to a few managers, including yours truly, who had agreed to take 100 cases of their crisps. I had my bike delivered directly to my house, and built it in the shed.

About a month later, head office got wind of the free bikes. Some stores had become greedy and grabbed two bikes, whilst others were smaller and hadn't been offered any. The area manager turned up one day and asked whether our store had received a bike. I told him it was on the top of the general office and would be raffled in the upcoming Carnival so that one of our customers would randomly receive it.

NO TEARS FOR TWENTY YEARS

That evening, I went to my shed. I dismantled the bike and next morning put it back in the office. Close call!

A couple of months later, the area manager was back in my store again and seemed excited. He had been promoted to director level and would be handing this store over to a different area manager. Ian Glen was to start the following week. His last words to me were, 'Take the bike home, Clive.'

Practically all stores had a Carnival Fund plus perks for managers. A manager at one store had two wristwatches – really top brass ones. When his deputy asked if he could have one, the manager replied, 'Yes, of course, I can sell it to you.'

Other stores had problems. Kings Heath Presto had no forklift truck driver in place for the weekend they opened. Instead, they let a Saturday lad step up, and he knocked a hole in the wall by the receiving bay.

My good salary and strong performance bonuses meant we were able to buy a static caravan. Previously, we'd enjoyed a heap of holidays in North Devon, but one year it had been rainier than we would have liked. With a static nearby, we could make use of every bit of good weather and not bother when it was wet. Abbot's Salford Caravan Park was less than 20 miles from Redditch. Its spot by the River Avon made it ideal for fishing, too.

It was on another drive that I first saw the site that would become the store that became my greatest success: Presto Evesham. I had heard that Alistair Grant had acquired eight Fine Fare stores, and one was in Evesham. New houses had been built and the town had been growing fast. The main competition was a Somerfield store in the town centre. The Fine Fare site was out of town, on Davies Road.

This time, I checked the site out on my own. It was just an empty building. Then I arranged a meeting with Regional Director Andy Morris in Salisbury and asked to be considered for the store general manager position in what I believed would be a flagship Presto store.

He thought I was out of my mind wanting to move again when Presto Sheldon, my current store, was doing so spectacularly well.

'You can have it if you want it,' he told me.

And I did!

I'd already found out that I derived great satisfaction from putting a team together from scratch. Here was another opportunity to do just that.

The first team members I recruited were Sue Lightheart, my people manager, and Jenny Stayley, who was working for Somerfield. Jenny had piercing steel-blue eyes. I hoped she might give me vital information on our competitor and gave her a cash office job, along with Tracey. Also fondly remembered are Ann on price marking; Penny, goods-in clerk; Sandra, checkout manager; Rob; James Ford on deliveries; Brenda on the information desk, who told me one of the best jokes I have ever heard and whose daughter Jane also worked for us; also Jane Hall, another lady whose shorthand came in useful at our weekly meetings; and Julie Parkes and Helen on bread and cakes. This fast-moving department could be a headache to keep on top of, yet these ladies did, to the point that wastage was usually under £20 per week.

The entire team were so loyal. I remember too Clive Cook on bakery, and Kent Ward, and Julie on fresh cream cakes – the fresh cream slices queen who had top sales in the company.

Carl and Steve also worked for me in Presto Evesham: Carl on grocery and Steve in the bakery.

The store was planned to have 15 checkouts, but I convinced senior management that we would cope with 11. This was very controversial. My thinking was that customers never get annoyed when they see you are doing your best. It was better to have all checkouts always staffed, even if queues were five deep, rather than risk not having sufficient staff to cover all 15. I also made sure I took on slightly less staff than needed – that way, if turnover went on to be less than expected, I wouldn't have to let people go. I was aware people had given up good jobs to come to work for Presto Evesham. I had seen it happen in other stores when, six months on, those same good people then found themselves out of work.

I was also determined that Presto Evesham would become part of the Cotswold community, and I became involved in every aspect of local life: Evesham United Football Club, the WI, local primary schools, Evesham Country Park, pubs, clubs, the *Evesham Journal* newspaper, local hotels and even Long Lartin Prison, a high-security prison some 3 miles away. You name it – fetes, charity do's, cup ties – and Presto Evesham would be involved in it.

A big money spinner was our close ties with Evesham United Football Club. Every week, they would have a £100 Presto voucher draw in the local *Journal* newspaper. It was a no-brainer. The lucky reader would have to spend the money in our store, and what an opportunity to win a customer from our competitors with our efforts in-store to make sure it was a good experience for that customer.

Mike McDonald, my deputy, and I would go to WI meetings about once a month and give talks about retail, and we would take food platters with us for the ladies to try. They proved very popular and could only take the store from strength to strength.

All this activity helped us become a top Argyll store in no time at all. As my first boss, Mr Tustin, once said to me, 'Everyone has to eat.' The members, pupils and workforce of those parks and schools, the prison and so forth were far more likely to switch their weekly shop to us because we'd shown such an interest in what was important to them. My thinking had paid off.

A promotion that we ran once was a 'freezer evening'. Jenny from Somerfield told me that they did them and they were very successful, so Mike and I organised one. All the frozen food reps gave us excellent prizes, but the winner was our butchery department. Geoff and his colleagues presented a whole lamb, pig joints and big packs of beef. We closed the store at 5 p.m., opened again at 6 p.m., and we had one hour to complete our point of sale and so forth. There was an advert in the *Journal* and we had distributed leaflets around the Cotswolds. The event was so busy that the police were called to Davies Road to control the traffic. From 6 p.m. until 9 p.m. we took £40,000. And yes, with 11 checkouts!

The link with Long Lartin was important because at that time they were one of the largest employers in the district. When the prison bakery had production problems, we supplied the bread. Believe me, that was a lot of bread. I was even given a tour of the prison. A guy came towards me on a landing complaining that there were not enough chairs in the television room. He was really pissed off when the governor told him I was not a government official. I was shown a cell where the walls were covered in oil paintings, and I made a comment about how nice they were. He replied saying how he had plenty of time to improve. He was an IRA terrorist on a very long sentence.

Evesham United Football Club proved a winner for the store. We sponsored their shirts, and our own football team then used their stadium as its home venue. And what a team Argyll United was! We began in Division Five, because we were 'new'. We then rose to Division One in four seasons. We also got involved in charity football matches against all-star celebrity teams. I remember a guy from the TV programme *London's Burning* who was a big hit with the ladies and two girls who were in *EastEnders* kicking off the match.

The year Argyll United did the double, that's to say when we won the championship and also the Bluck Cup, I was so proud that I put on a show for the lads at Abbot's Salford Caravan Park Club. By this point, Beryl and I owned a caravan on the park, so it was easy for me to arrange things.

Alistair Grant always followed our progress.

I hired a Black Country comedian, Tony Palmer, and two strippers. The biggest issue was the two ladies couldn't find the caravan park and called at a local pub to ask for directions. The night at the caravan park was 'men only', and so our ladies – including Beryl – had gone to the Golden Cross pub that night. You could scarcely make it up. At the Golden Cross pub, the people the strippers asked where the Abbot's Salford Caravan Park was were Beryl and Sue, my staff supervisor, and Sandra Rogers, whose husband, Jim, was also at the show.

Well! Neither of us had told our wives about the strippers. Now they knew, they . . . got into Sue's car and drove straight to the club!

The wives arrived just as Rudy – Sue's husband – was enjoying one of the girls sitting on his lap. She had dipped one of her breasts into his beer and was now inviting him to lick the foam. Beryl and co didn't come in; they peeped in through the clubroom curtains.

Good fun, in my view. We also had a whip-round to pay the girls that bit extra, and in return one chap, Steve, a builder who lived at the top of the lane, was selected for very special treatment. He had brewer's droop after way too much beer, and possibly didn't get quite the value he anticipated. But fair play. He stood on stage, starkers, threw his arms up in the air and shouted, 'Yeah!' That, plus a lit cigarette and a whip that is inappropriate to detail in this book, are still spoken about today. Nice one, Mike Mc.

I also remember very fondly the many parties we held at our home in Redditch. One New Year's Eve we had 63 people.

We fitted everyone in by temporarily removing all the internal doors (we stored them in the garage) and spilling out into the garden at midnight, when it was especially lively. I went into the front garden to fire my shotgun into the night sky. (Note: I no longer have this shotgun!)

Some parties were fancy dress. I am thinking of Ken (Sheldon) as Hilda Ogden from *Coronation Street*, a young lad as Boy George, and Martin Downes and Rose, both from Presto Evesham, who came as skeletons. I can vividly remember Tracey (cash office, Evesham) dressed as a police woman, going outside and flagging down a police car! In good spirits, the officers came indoors to see what was going on and ended up enjoying the food and music.

I was a lousy dancer, but could move well enough to my 'favourite', 'Mississippi' by Pussycat. I would sing too. Crap really. My party piece was to sing Elvis Presley's 'Wooden Heart' – in German! – to Beryl.

Being the general store manager of Evesham was the most satisfying period of my retail career. As before, I committed to giving 120 per cent back to colleagues who committed 100 per cent to me. I told the staff that if they needed any food, I would make sure they got it, but if they stole anything and were caught, they would have to go. No second chance.

My straight-talking approach was rewarded by the lowest staff turnover in the company and very low sickness levels. I'd tailor specific small rewards. For example, I gave the night-crew women a bunch of flowers on Sunday morning. I also accepted that Ann W sometimes came in a few minutes late. When a few members of staff made their cross feelings about this known, I had a ready answer: 'If you want to be a few minutes late, then go ahead. But make sure you work over for as long as it takes to finish your work on that day.' No more was said.

I did have more to think about, however, when I received a phone call to say that Ann's boyfriend, Dave, who was my merchandising manager, was in hospital with a punctured lung. Ann and Dave had had an argument at home, and, it was alleged, she had put a knife in his back. I saw Dave in hospital and he was one forgiving guy. Ann (who was much older than him) had endured tragedy with her first husband, who was a telephone engineer. He had been killed whilst repairing telephone wires in Headless Cross, Redditch. A wire was hanging in the road and whilst there had been a guy watching for traffic, a horrific accident occurred as a car drove past and caught onto the wire. This pulled Ann's husband from the top of the pole into the road with so much force that it killed him.

After the punctured lung incident, Dave wanted to let the matter with his injury drop, and no one was charged.

John Clements joined the store as a young lad. I could see he had potential, but needed to tackle tougher tasks if he were to develop. Working nights, I thought, would do the trick. District Personnel Manager Sue wasn't pleased. John was only 17. But he did nights and, I am sure as a result of it, went on to do really well in his retail career. He settled into management, as did Steve Guoite, another lad who started out under my wing. He is now doing well in Australia having a senior position with Woolworths, I believe. Another Jon – Jon

Roberts – gave me a scare when he made the *Midlands Today* news. I was watching at home when a report was broadcast showing a man on a skydive who had broken his ankle on landing. Jon. I couldn't be cross that he needed time off work, though, as the skydive had raised a good amount for charity.

Across the late 1980s and early 1990s, retail was a fast-moving, six-days-a-week industry. The Presto Evesham Saturday night final figures were always eagerly awaited. When they were spectacular – which they so often were – we'd celebrate by opening a box of red and white wines that was kept behind the checkouts for just such news. There was always a small disagreement between myself and Geoff, the butcher's manager. It was about till difference. That's to say the difference in pounds between the value from the meat department and the checkout figures of said items, produced by my weekend cash office girl, Tracey. The difference could be as much as £500. I would send Geoff to recheck his stocks. If he thought he was having one over on me by putting across a flaky figure, I was light years ahead of him!

I liked Geoff well enough, though, and every Sunday, we enjoyed
a roast in our kitchen at Redditch, courtesy of his department – another little sweetener in a general store manager's life. For my part, I would send a bottle of wine to the butchery staff on special occasions. But I had to be on my metal. Just the once, I believe they took a second bottle from the shelf. From that point, I always made a mark on the label so that no further sherry could be substituted from the stock floor.

NO TEARS FOR TWENTY YEARS

My years at Presto Evesham were, as I have said, the best years of my working life. In 1986, the store was awarded Top Store of the Year Award, and that was out of all UK Presto stores. As soon as Area Manager Phil 'Under the Wispa Wrappers' Cooke gave me the news, I was thrilled to share it with my staff. The Top Store Award wouldn't have happened without them.

I also received personal awards, signed by the board members, for generating one million pounds of profit. To mark what was clearly a stellar moment, I was presented with a magnum of fine champagne, which was personally labelled with my name, the date and that I had achieved that million milestone. It's the truth that many store general managers could spend their entire career without receiving one. Store managers were presented with one every time a million of net profit was reached.

I was presented with five over the years.

Enough said!

That doesn't mean every moment at work was sparkling. I recall being told to expect four visitors to the store – I didn't know the purpose of the visit. I assumed it was that they were from a division at head office and wanted to see how we got our excellent results. As I showed them around, I pointed out all the little things that we did differently at this store. I was happy that, as they enjoyed a coffee in the canteen, they could see the brilliant staff atmosphere at my store. I also saw that they had a copy of a profit-and-loss sheet.

As they left, one said: 'I can see why we were sent to this store.'

Again, I took that to be a compliment.

The next day, District Manager Trevor Preece summoned me to the regional office in Bristol. To my shock, I was told that I needed to write a letter to Sir Alistair Grant, CEO of Argyll Foods, to apologise for the way that I handled the visit. The people who had come to the store weren't Argyll people, but investors with large shareholdings in Argyll. I replied that if a different style of visit had been needed, then I should have been informed these people were investors. I would have certainly tailored my tour to ensure they came away wanting to invest more.

Shortly after, Argyll bought Safeway and decided to convert all Prestos into Safeway. Conversion teams began the slow process. Typically, what happened was that existing Safeway managers were put temporarily into Presto stores and the existing Presto managers were sent on training courses. In 99 per cent of cases, those former Presto managers never got to return to their original store.

I was determined that this wouldn't happen to me, and, with the excellent performance figures of my Evesham store, I was able to go on a training course to learn 'Safeway-ways' then return to the same store.

There were differences between the two brands – for example, Presto did not have pharmacies whereas most Safeway stores did. But I believe that 'retail is detail', and so much of the training I was compelled to go on I did not need.

At the Retail Career Development Centre run by Safeway, most of the course was office-based. But one day we stepped outside – onto an assault course! This was held at a specialist outward-bound centre and included a rope walk across a ravine. Another challenge was when you had to use a different single piece of rope to swing between two trees.

What all this had to do with running a supermarket, I did not know. I can only assume it was about teamwork and the skill of encouraging colleagues who felt out of their depth.

We were divided into two teams, with around 15 people in each. I was in my 40s and felt an old man compared to many of the younger managers. There was a net under the rope to stop you from going into the ravine, but as I stepped onto the rope bridge, how I felt my heart pound! I was so nervous. I got to the last step and, just as I thought I would fall, I felt the reassuring grip of a team member – this lovely guy who was ex-army. Teamwork in action.

It was true enough that afterwards it did feel good to have pushed myself and been successful.

The opposing team were shocked that I had completed the task. We won overall, too. I think the guy doing the marking knocked the other team down for their attitude. They had said things like, 'Oh, Clive won't be able to do the river walk.' In working life, you have to be encouraging to everyone.

I will say, however, that Safeway training methods were the best in the retail industry.

To complete the conversion training, I had to sit a RCDC test. Passing this wasn't a problem. Area Manager Norman Cooper phoned me at the store to tell me my result. I passed with a B. Having run stores for more than three decades, I can't say I was surprised!

On the shop floor, however, it took a great deal of hard work to get our Safeway results up to the position where the Presto ones had been. Safeway stores used methods that were poor at controlling both stock levels and waste. But within weeks, I had found ways to work with their systems that meant we were a strong performer once more.

Shortly afterwards, Sir Alistair agreed to my request that Evesham needed a larger store.

In 1987, Argyll purchased what was then a field of sprouts, and turned it into a new, much larger Safeway supermarket, just a quarter of a mile down the road from the previous one.

For some months I was flitting between the new site and the old one, which was now being run by Peter Burgess.

Pete had been my deputy at Davies Road for a while. He was a great organiser and planner – and also a good footballer (now a globe-trotter) along with a few other lads who had taken the Argyll United team to dizzy heights. Let me name them here: Dave Cuneen, Kevin Hanagan, Mike McDonald, Rob Pratley and Neil 'My Ball' Smith.

Shortly before opening day, the car park was being completed. I drove in, and my exhaust scraped one of the 'sleeping policeman' humps that had been installed to keeps car speeds low.

I told the project manager, Peter, that he needed to lower the bumps. If my car had scraped its exhaust, what would happen to cars laden down with the weekly shop? Almost a week passed, but nothing was done.

'I think we should wait and see,' he said.

'I will organise a jackhammer and reduce them myself,' I blasted.

By the next time I drove in, they had been reduced in height.

Regional Director Martin Flaherty visited the old store in Davies Road on its final Friday night and commented that it looked like a store that was about to close down. 'Even so,' I told him, 'the store will take more money this week than last week.' He bet me £5 that I would be wrong.

I was not. We'd cashed up the previous week a day earlier, so it would be a comparison of six days then, with seven now. 'Thanks for the fiver,' I told him happily.

The new Safeway store was positioned on the town's link road and surrounded by a growing housing estate. It took off where the previous one left off – with happy staff who worked hard, received a simple thank you from management and then came back to do it all again the next day.

Another funny happening was a guy calling in to the store one evening and starting a dust-up with one of my managers, Rob. He thought he was Andy.

Shortly after opening, we had a high-profile visit from Sir Alistair Grant and Safeway directors. The store was packed with Saturday shoppers. One director, Pat Kieran, made the comment that the store looked like 'Paddy's market' because it wasn't tidy and some counters were piled high.

I wasn't having this!

'The problem is that you may never have seen a store so busy nor customer trolleys so full,' I told him sharply.

I was also able to point out how the store hadn't been built with a letter box, and this was swiftly rectified.

It was in 1995/6 that Area Manager Phil Coyle came to visit and suggested we sit in my office. This was unusual – Phil and myself both liked to be out on the shop floor, discussing issues etc.

'Clive,' he told me, 'this is serious. Safeway are to offer a deal to everyone over the age of 50. Redundancy. Early retirement. Call it what you will. Everyone over 50 will be eligible to receive an enhanced pension and a generous package. Details will be sent in due course.'

Everyone over 50! With a birthdate of 1942, that was me, of course, and also a good many of my colleagues with a wealth of experience who would jump at the deal.

I felt total shock. I had worked for the same company (under a host of different company names) for almost 40 years. Could I leave it now?

Once the full financial details arrived, it was a no-brainer. I and practically everyone over 50 took the deal. When I informed Safeway that I would take the offer, they asked me to stay on for a further 12 months to ensure a smooth handover.

When I next met Sir Alistair, I told him that this policy could be a mistake. All his experienced people would go. The stores would not run well at all. And how true this turned out. Within a few years of our exit, Safeway began to fail and so Morrisons was able to take them over.

It was some time before the takeover bid when I found myself on a plane travelling to Gambia chatting to a pleasant lady in the next seat. I told her about my experiences with Safeway and how they operated. 'Why not write to Ken Morrison then?' she said. 'I'm a board member of Morrisons myself and I find what you say really interesting!'

I did write to Sir Ken, telling him how when there was a high-profile visit, stores would load all their pallets of excess stock onto a depot vehicle to take it away from the store, then bring it back once the visit was over. This way, the important visitors would think stock control was way better than it was. In my letter, I put to him my view that Safeway were 'all gloss and no content'. He did write back to me, thanking me for my letter and wishing me all the best for the future.

Little did I know then, of course, that . . . jump forward 13 years and I would be a Morrisons employee myself! Funny how life spins around, isn't it?

The proudest moment of my retail career, Presto Evesham, Top Store in the entire country, look at all those happy faces

George, my Boss from my early retail days, catch up now and again, and put Retail to rights. nice day in Lyme.

The all time greats "Argyll United" will never forget, how proud they made me, (Presto Evesham) Double winners ,

Ken and wife Janet , another Fancy Dress n/y Party, at our house in Redditch do not think they missed one, RIP Ken,

Cynthia, with nanny Beryl, deep in thought in the Gambia She loves her Nanny.

Steve with Charlie, ("his pet Jackdaw") 1978 ?

"Welcome to the Millionaires Club" you got one every time you made a million pound profit, i had 4 in 2 yrs, " Safeway"

11: ADVENTURES IN AFRICA

It was November 1989. 'Steve,' I said, passing across an atlas of the world as we sat on the sofa at home. 'Put a pin in where you want to go and we shall. Just me and you.'

Gambia, where the pin landed, changed our lives.

It could have been a disaster as we headed off for two weeks at the Atlantic Hotel, Banjul, in Gambia's capital city. It changed all our lives.

Steve loved Gambia so much that within a couple of years he made the place his home. Gambia also became a second home for Beryl and me, and remains so more than 20 years on.

We flew for six hours with Thomas Cook and when the plane doors opened at Banjul Airport, it felt like being in a fire. The dry heat was incredible.

We spent our time at the hotel, around the pool, on the beach and also seeing wildlife. I remember owls by night and beautiful jewel-bright birds by day. Everyone seemed to be on the wacky backy, but that didn't bother me. Three locals, Malic Faal and Kebba (the latter now deceased), and Seedy took us fishing. In time we would also meet Tijan, who took us birdwatching.

The hotel was amongst the best in the country. Around that time the pop group UB40 even went there to shoot a video! A local fisherman called Lucky Man built a boat and named it after the band. He'd bring it up from the shore each evening and drop it into the hotel swimming pool, just for show.

Prices for food and drinks were cheap, but not exceptionally so. That first year, we got 11 of the local currency, dalasi (D), to the pound. Today it is 79 to the pound!

I met Ferry Kazna on that first trip, too – he was raising money for the charity Schools for Progress and I said I would help. He told me about a school in Saba that needed a generator so that it could have electricity. Having electricity in a school doesn't just mean light; it enables the school to generate income from renting the classrooms in the evenings to local tailors etc.

'I will raise £5,000,' I told him, 'and then return.'

Poverty was widespread in Gambia and only hotels and official places had electricity (via their own generators). Schools certainly didn't. Back home, I rallied Presto staff and friends to contribute using the incentive that for every £20 raised, they would be entered into a raffle with the prize of a free trip to Gambia to be involved with the handover and installation of the generator. I also approached a local school, Harvington First School, and the head teacher, Marcia, got behind my project. The school raised money and in return, Safeway Evesham later helped them to raise money for a school library.

We met the £5,000 target, no issue. I also managed to get £5,000 worth of vegetable seeds, courtesy of Ron Joysnon, head of produce for Presto at the time. I distributed the seeds to schools across Gambia after consulting government officials.

Before *that* return trip, however, I wanted to take two other people over to Gambia: Steve's brother and his mum. I knew Beryl would either love or hate the heat and the very different way of life in Gambia. There wouldn't be a half measure.

I honestly didn't think she would take to it – Beryl likes things to be scrupulously clean and orderly. But she loved it! So much so that we began to talk seriously about how much time we could spend there. We'd sit at our favourite restaurant, Scala, in the Senegambia area, and think how lovely life was with no work and just enjoying ourselves in a beautiful place.

First, though, we had to organise the winner's trip to Gambia from all that fundraising. I knew how much difference the £5,000 we had now raised would make to Saba First School, and I was eager to put my promise into action.

At Presto, and to my great surprise, the first three winners drawn out of the hat didn't want to go. They worried about mosquitoes, and they didn't want to get vaccines (yellow fever and tetanus). Finally, it was decided that it would be Miriam, the manager of the café, and Sandra from checkout (who took her husband, Jim, along too). We had an amazing time and, possibly as a direct result of that trip, Sandra and Jim became our closest friends for many, many years.

We travelled to the school, pausing on the journey to drink coffee straight from tin cans! We travelled along the River Gambia on a very unstable ferry to get to the North Bank Division of the country. Then, it was onto rough dirt tracks.

They were so happy to see us and to thank us for the money. Jim, a builder, also helped create a new schoolroom by laying a couple of blocks, which were made by locals. On the way back, the journey turned into chaos. The ferry boat got stuck on the river and then another ferry that came to the rescue got stuck too. At one point, Miriam needed a wee and all she could do was hold on to us with one hand and do the business, crouching inches off the back of the ferry. We weren't on dry land until 2 a.m. the next day.

That day, we went to a restaurant to recover and celebrate. Jim thought the staff didn't understand his order of chicken and chips and repeated it. Finally, he got three portions!

Back home, we planned our next family trip. We honestly didn't want to holiday anywhere else. Within a few years, we had decided two weeks in Gambia wasn't enough; we needed to stay for two months at a time.

By this point, my work situation had changed, as I had left Safeway and begun working for Neil Allen, the top man at Allen's Caravans whose sites included Abbot's Salford. Beryl had started working for him, too. So we were able to do just that, and stay for two months at a time by dint of my working seven days a week for 10 months and receiving a little over two months off on full pay.

It was whilst we were in the Scala restaurant that we met John Baldwin, who owned a small holiday complex called Karadula Lodge. It was 1998 and we struck a deal with him to build a a two-bedroom lodge for us within the complex. We paid £14,000 and the agreement was that we could use the property for three months a year for 10 years. There was a clause that the owner would buy back from us for £7,000 after five years, if we asked him to, or he could make us quit if he so decided.

Five years on, and we decided to move to a bigger place. In 2003 we went on a safari trip. It was brilliant and we saw wild pigs, crocodiles and lots of monkeys. On the way back from Sanyang, and travelling through an area called Brufut, we saw a sign advertising 'Taff houses for sale'. We stopped and met Taff who showed us a bungalow under construction. The lady who had originally paid a deposit for this bungalow could no longer complete.

'Let's tell John that we want to leave Karadula, sell our caravan in Abbot's Salford and use the funds to buy this,' I said to Beryl. We didn't need the caravan because we were living in a cottage at Weir Meadow in Evesham, belonging to Neil Allen. It came with my job of running the site.

With Steve living full-time in Gambia and in a seemingly secure job as a chef at Kololi Hotel, we both liked the idea of having somewhere more spacious and permanent to stay when we came over.

We paid £35,000 for 4 Jamma Avenue, Brufut Gardens, which is the splendid bungalow property we own today. We also helped to fund a place for Steve on the same site. He designed the layout of his property and was able to oversee it with care.

That said, Gambian building can be a tad slow. The first time Beryl went out to see our bungalow, work hadn't been completed and she had to stay at a hotel paid for by Taff, the builder!

Lots of Brits live on the estate and we pay for 24/7 security organised by Solice and Skiaka. Solice sadly died. Now it is Skiaka and Modu. Security is an absolute essential. Gambia is a very poor country and people are desperate. But people are very friendly, too, and a lot of Gambians love us to bits, especially Beryl and Steve. Whenever I leave the compound, I make sure to wear my oldest, tattiest clothes. That way I am not stopped by the locals. Those who don't know me must look and think, *Poor sod.*

In January to March, there is no other place that we want to be. Outside of those times, the weather is too humid for us. There is also the 15 feet of rainfall that lands in July and August: too much for Beryl and me, but not for Steve.

Life out there for him, however, hasn't been without perils – at one point he nearly died from malaria. Thank goodness Steve was young, fit and strong and so recovered. Dr Musa, who treated him, told me that if he had not been so fit and healthy he would have certainly not pulled through. In Gambia, as it is throughout Africa, malaria is the biggest single killer.

In time, Steve met a girl who was from Zaire. Barvie is around 10 years younger than him. They faced tragedy when her twin pregnancy ended in the stillbirth of one baby and the death within days of the second child. I organised a headstone. There was no coffin. Steve bought silks to wrap the babies in before they were buried, but these were stolen at the hospital, so he bought more.

The people out there are also so poor that they will eat rats etc. Once, after a storm, Beryl and I saw a rat the size of a cat (called a *Drimmo*) that had drowned and lay in a gutter. Ten minutes later, it was gone. A local would have taken it for food.

In December 2006, Steve and Barvie had a daughter, Cynthia. This time, Barvie was in hospital for only the minimum amount of time, before going to a relative who looked after her and the baby in those early weeks. Watching our grandaughter grow up into a smart, happy girl has been one of life's joys. It was, of course, another reason to keep coming out to Gambia each year.

Strange story: Barvie and Cynthia were out one morning, on the way to see Steve who by then was manager at a fitness centre. The road was packed. Yahya Jammeh, the then former military chief who became president of Gambia, was expected to pass in a cavalcade. As he did, he stopped and handed out a few T-shirts to people in the crowd (which is what he usually did), and then he pointed to Cynthia, then aged three.

'Bring me that child,' he said. With no choice, Barvie handed her daughter over. Jammeh pronounced how beautiful she was, and returned her to Barvie with D10,000 in cash. Today, D10,000 is worth about £130.

In 2013, Steve and Barvie had a beachside wedding. Our friends Sandra and Jim were there – by this time Sandra and Jim had bought an apartment nearby! In my speech, I said, 'You probably won't remember this day, Cynthia, but . . . I always shall.'

Cynthia went to Sebec International School and really shone and made lots of friends too. She's such a clever girl.

During our months in Gambia, she would come to stay with us for Fridays, Saturdays and Sundays. We loved it! Beryl spoils her rotten, like she does her other grandchildren.

Cynthia was around nine when they moved to the UK. The Christmas before the family moved, she wrote to Santa: 'What I want for Christmas is to move to the UK. Please send your answer to Nanny and Grandad in England!'

Barvie had a friend in Chard, Somerset, and she and Cynthia moved there. Steve joined them after a few months of organising the sale of their home and safe passage for their beloved cats. Steve has always been ready to help animals in need, and the first cat he had in Gambia found him. The cat, whom he called Muss, was trapped under the engine of his four-by-four. He heard a miaow, and there it was. A kitten. There was no way to trace its original home and it was most likely to have been a stray, anyhow. In time, Steve went on to adopt two cats. Marrian and Kiko returned to the UK; sadly, Muss had passed away earlier. Steve now works at a hospital as a porter and Cynthia is doing her A-levels.

Whilst his wife and daughter haven't been back to Africa, Steve and me went for a two-week fishing trip in November 2023. Our aim is always to head to Battakuncu Beach and land butterfish, or to go out on the boat with Seedy to catch barracuda. Steve's cooking skills are always appreciated!

GWhen Beryl and I stay in Gambia, we always have a wonderful time. We keep a Jeep Cherokee so we can get out and about. Gambian drivers are notorious – they keep on going, even if cattle appear on the road, which they often do. There are so many accidents. Once, when we were on a side-road, Beryl's sunglasses flew off. I stopped to get them, then we saw a wild boar come out of the bushes. We left the glasses on the road!

Another time, Beryl and Carl were smoking in the back of the jeep. They had put a towel over their heads to keep off the sun and dust, only the towel caught fire. It didn't go out until they banged the towel ferociously.

We have many friends in Gambia: June, Frank, Christine, Margaret 75-year-old lady, Barbara, who had a very young Gambian lover. Once, she told us her brother was coming to visit and she felt it was vital that he didn't hear about her boyfriend. She had fixed this by taking her brother on a very luxurious river cruise for the duration of his visit and she paid for us to come along with her, too. Great fun. We swam with dolphins (well, her brother did).

We always remember those in Gambia who have so much less than us. During the months we spend in the UK, we get together boxes of clothes and learning materials for children. We then get these shipped across to Gambia alongside the clothes and provisions we send over for ourselves. When we arrive, we give them to local charities, such as SOS Children's Village in Bakoteh. We receive some wonderful thank you letters. In 2019, SOS director, Haddy Njie Touray, wrote, 'May God bless and reward you abundantly in the noble work you are undertaking.'

In the 20 years we have been staying in Gambia, we have seen change. There has been more building – of roads and homes. I have also noticed there are far fewer European tourists these days. Fewer English, Germans and Swedes in particular. But who knows, this could get better, which I dearly hope it does, as I want to keep visiting our second home for as long as possible. It's not nice getting old and not being able to do things, or wishing you could do things that you used to be able to do.

Still aint lost it, Loved my Catty, even in Africa.

Malic Faal, Steves best mate in Gambia, i had so much fun with him, and his family

Beryl, Sandra, Jim, and Tijan, Termite Hill, (15 ft high) Gambia. Happy Days

Barvie, Steve and Cynthia, Gambia. in one of the many bars on The Strip.

Steve and Carl , Brufut beach, Gambia Carl is at his best when hes got a fire going

Battacuncu, Gambia. take care.(Python)

Carl, Posing with my Captain fish, Gungur, the gambia They all thought i was stuck in sea weed. nice one,

12: WHEN ONE DOOR CLOSES ...

As soon as I knew that my days with Safeway were numbered, I spoke to Neil Allen. 'You can have a job as a gardener right away,' Neil told me.

The very week I ceased to work at Safeway, I began. The next week, Neil asked me to step up to be site warden. I wouldn't get an increase in salary, but after a few months, I would no longer be charged for ground rent, electricity and gas. I had my Safeway pension coming in by now, so it seemed a very reasonable deal, plus I would have the benefit of enjoying a job and lifestyle that kept me close to nature – something you didn't get to see when you put in long, long hours inside a supermarket.

That Christmas, I was in the site office on gas duty (helping owners who wanted gas), when Neil and his younger brother, Mark, put a leaflet about Weir Meadow Caravan and Holiday Park on the counter.

'Would you like to manage this for me?' Neil asked me.

'But it's not yours,' I said, checking out a different company's logo on the leaflet.

'It is now!' came the reply. 'I've just bought it.'

'Go and have a look at the site,' he continued. 'There's a nice cottage you and Beryl could live in.'

It felt like a dream opportunity.

Just a year or so previously, I'd felt on the scrapheap at 55 years old. Now I was being offered a great place to live along the River Avon in Evesham.

There were 150 static caravans, 15 holiday lets, five flats, three chalets and around 100 or so spots for touring caravans. I could certainly manage this – I had run a multimillion-pound store with dozens of employees. This position would also give me scope for selling more statics.

We kept our house in Redditch, and whilst I stayed full-time in Willowcroft Cottage at Weir Meadow, Beryl came down at weekends. During the week, she was on call to look after our school-age grandchildren, Lauren and Adam. Carl and his then wife, Lisa, were both at work, putting in long hours. Lisa was a teacher and Carl was liquor manager at Safeway, Redditch, so Beryl was often needed. In the school holidays, we'd take both of them on trips. Adam, who has autism, had a keen interest in Lego at one point, so a trip to Legoland was a must. We also went to zoos and parks. Being grandparents was – and continues to be – tremendous. I have always had plenty of energy and even after being on my feet at work all week, I still had plenty to spare to play with Adam and Lauren. Today, Lauren has followed her mum into teaching, whilst Adam works as a glass engraver.

Beryl was approaching 50 by now, but when we moved into the cottage at Weir Meadow, she didn't take it easy, not even for a moment. At the weekends, she joined the Weir Meadow team responsible for the shower and toilet blocks and holiday caravans. Helping her were Anne and Mary – great ladies – plus Phil, who combined handyman tasks with being a salesman. I also took on Brian (Mucka Bri) to help out. A fellow Wombourne guy, he lived in his tourer before buying a static caravan. Sue, who had also worked for me at Presto/Safeway, worked in the office at Weir Meadow.

Managing a holiday home site, I found out to my delight, was no different to being an SGM in retail. It was about attention to detail and serving the customers.

Neil went on to buy a further three caravan sites – The Springs, Barton and one inBidford-on-Avon. With Mucka Bri's help, we were able to look after them all. During our time at Weir Meadow, we even won the Evesham in Bloom competition.

Neil was so good to me that it felt OK to work seven days a week. The deal was that during the closed season, which ran from January to March, I would take eight weeks off but receive full pay. This, of course, enabled me to stay in Gambia over the winter.

Most noteworthy during my Weir Meadow years were the 2007 floods. Following the heaviest rainfall in 200 years, the river rose 19 feet.

'We're trapped in the upstairs bedroom,' I told the 999 operator. All we could see from our window were gas bottles bobbing on the surface of water that seemed almost as high as our first-floor windows, and, in the distance, static caravans that had been ripped from their spot now torn apart as they were carried along the enlarged river by the sheer force of the current.

When the flooding started, we had swiftly evacuated the residents from their caravans. Up in the cottage, we wrongly thought we would be OK. It had been so quick, but the water had risen across the entire downstairs.

An hour later, we still hadn't been rescued.

I rang again, only to be told that there *had* been a rescue party. They'd come to the wrong side of the cottage and hadn't seen us.

'It will have to be rescue by helicopter,' I was told. One look at Beryl and I knew that was not an option. No way would she go into a helicopter.

It was agreed that we would be evacuated by boat instead. The boat arrived under the bedroom window and because the water was so very high by now, it was hardly a climb down at all as we lowered ourselves from the bedroom window and into the boat.

The rescue team took us to the top of Port Street, which was the first spot high enough to not be submerged. Crowds had gathered to watch. First to greet us was Julie Parkes, a former Presto colleague. She soon had a cup of tea for us both.

It was sad beyond belief when, once the floods had subsided, we returned to view the cottage. It didn't matter about the furniture or furnishings that were ruined. It was – and remains – a huge upset that all our photographs were destroyed. These included irreplaceable photos of Mom, Dad, and my brothers when we were children. Beryl also lost many of her family photos. My sharp-as-a-tack memory means that in my head I can still see today how we all looked; but – oh – that is not the same as having a real photograph to display and cherish. I, rather than Irwin or Larry, had been the keeper of our family photographs. Now they were gone.

I managed to rescue one photograph, of Mom and Dad watching the Wembley FA Cup Final when Wolves were playing Leicester and Dad's friend Billy Wright was team captain. But that was about it. Repairs to the cottage took a long time, so it was good that we still had our Redditch house.

In early 2008, Neil Allen died and we attended his funeral. The wake, which was held at Wootton Hall, was a lively affair as Neil had been a very popular guy. There was no shortage of alcohol served, although I had none as I was still successfully fighting the demon drink. Afterwards, I ended up putting Beryl to bed at Weir Meadow.

I was now 66, so past official retirement age but, of course, still putting in a very decent amount of work each week. It felt right, however, to think about the years ahead in terms of where we lived. Beryl had arthritis and, in time, perhaps she might prefer to live in a one-storey place. We had loved the freedom that you feel when you live on a site where there are permanent static homes. Should we do this full-time? We decided to sell Redditch and buy a place on another site Neil owned. Wootton Wawen has around 250 retirement homes and we chose a lovely plot near to a stream and wooded area. I knew there would be plenty of birds and other wildlife to watch.

After Neil's death, full control of Allen's Caravans passed to his brother, Mark, and sister, Julie. I continued in my job and, when that November came, I said my usual, 'Farewell.

See you in two months!' as Beryl and I headed across to Gambia.

Little did I know that on my return all would not be well and that, yet again, a new chapter in my life would begin.

Mucka Bri and myself, with the "Evesham in Bloom" Trophy three yrs on the trot, Weir Meadow H/Park, lovely Guy.

Day after the floods Weir Meadow holiday park nothing survived, but no lives were lost. 2007.?

Beryl and Lauren,(Carls Daughter) Abbotts Salford, Carravan Park , great days , and nights.

Steve with his friend "Kebba" taken in "Ali Barbers" Gambia another who was taken early R I P Kebba

The Cottage, that was our home at Weir Meadow, top right window we were rescued from during the Floods, "Scary"

Anne, who worked, with Jan and Beryl at Weir Meadow H/Park (Evesham) all perfectionists at their job. happy days.

13: ALCOHOL AND OTHER ADDICTIONS: THEIR ROLE IN MY STORY

In the last chapter, I mentioned that at Neil Allen's wake I didn't drink. In truth, it wasn't just at that occasion, because I had stopped in 1997. I had stopped abruptly, because that is the only way that someone who has been addicted to alcohol, as I was, could ever do it.

I am proud to state that, as I write this in 2023, I have not had a drink in more than 25 years. It has not been easy. But, after such a long time now, I am confident that I will always stay as I am now, although I do still fight it.

Here is the story to detail in full my hidden addiction to alcohol.

I first drank alcohol when I was around 13. I'd visit Uncle Arthur and have a look in the 'bogey hole' as I called the place under the stairs where he stored damson, potato and carrot home brew. It was meant to be wine, but tasted more like whisky. I'd unscrew the bottle tops, then sneak a little from each bottle. A few bottles. A sip from each. Mom did his washing and I'd take it back to the Wodehouse, so I often visited. Mom would have a beer with her mate Clara Bow at the Vine, but no one was a big drinker in our family. Arthur drank his home brews steadily over months, and also had 'a nut brown' beer on Saturday nights. So there is no family reason why I alone would become addicted to alcohol, except that I have an addictive nature.

When I became a store manager at supermarkets, the company reps who called at the stores would sometimes give me bottles of alcohol. Pretty soon I was getting home from work, grabbing a half-pint glass, filling it with three-quarters whisky, a quarter Coke. I was never fall-down drunk; I just felt relaxed. It was my way of unpacking the day. I didn't even get hangovers to slow me down.

As my dependency on alcohol grew, I'd keep Special Brew in the car and if it had been a really hard day and it was now 11 p.m., I would drink one on the way home from Evesham to Redditch, tossing the empty out of the window.

In those days, managers used to dress very smartly for work. One evening, I was wearing my usual white shirt with a black bow tie when I stopped at a fish and chip shop in Astwood Bank, Redditch.

'Are you going someplace nice?' the girl serving asked.

'Just back from work,' I replied.

'Pull the other one,' she said.

If I had been pulled up by the police the way I was dressed, I would have been breathalysed and that would have been it.

At that time, Beryl was manager at Kwik Save and also did long hours, so I did the cooking at home. On days off, I'd drink a bottle of wine whilst I was preparing the meal.

When we were in Gambia, I'd drink JulBrew and sometimes 'jungle juice' – a drink made from palm trees, that was collected from the tree sap by locals called 'wine tappers'.

Loads of times I tried to stop. I'd eat bags of crisps in the evenings and in my car, off my lap, instead of beers. But it didn't last. The lure of alcohol that I didn't even have to pay for was too strong.

It was the same with cigarettes. I'd quit, then restart. Finally, one New Year's party I did it. I'd said my usual 'I'm going to stop' then lit up again. I was dancing with Yvonne from next door when I casually lit up without thinking, and just minutes after I was saying that I would stop.

'You'll never stop,' she said, reasonably enough.

I took the lit cigarette from my mouth and stubbed it out. And from that point, I have never smoked again. It was like that part of me was finished. Beryl still smokes, but it doesn't bother me.

I have known from my teens that I have an addictive personality. A habit takes hold, and I can't stop. My first 'addiction' was betting on horses, as I've written about in an earlier chapter.

I don't know why I stopped smoking that New Year's night. It was several years before I left Presto/Safeway. It actually wasn't that hard in the end. No idea why.

Drinking – or rather not drinking – is less easy.

I finally and successfully managed to stop drinking within a year of retiring from Safeway. Thinking about what it might go on to do to my health had never been a sufficient motivator, so I focused on how, with my free supply dried up, I would now have to start paying for it.

Incredibly, this approach worked. In the evenings, I replaced alcohol with chocolate. I'd eat an enormous bar in one hit. Weeks, then months passed without a drink. But I was, and always will be, a recovering alcoholic.

I didn't seek outside support and, to be honest, I didn't have any physical symptoms or issues. Perhaps that's because I didn't have any health issues when I did drink. That doesn't mean that it has been or continues to be easy. I don't trust myself to 'have just one' and, whilst I am OK with keeping it in the cupboard (I have those special bottles of champagne I was awarded at work, still untouched), I don't feel comfortable around alcohol.

At 81, I simply don't need to make life harder for myself and my family, although to be honest, Beryl would not let me!

Trevor and Janet, and Beryl, great times, RIP Trevor.

Sharon (Larrys Daughter) better known as Jesty Guest giving Steve a clout,

Atlantic Hotel , Banjul, Steve,s, early Friends in the Gambia 1988

Day out at Lynmouth, Devon, Watersmeet, one of our favourite places, on holiday, Steves getting a Big Boy.

Paul (Paulines son) Dean (Trevors son) with Carl n Steve, Cam/Close, Redditch. the night they got locked in the Garage

14: RETURNING TO THE SHOP FLOOR

We'd unpacked from our Gambia trip and the next morning I went to the office at Allen's Caravans to report in for duty and ask what next.

'We have nothing for you,' I was told by Allens.

I could not believe what I heard! I had been working for Allen's for over 13 years. Only now, it seemed, they had got someone else to do my role whilst we were away on an agreed absence. I went straight to a solicitor and, in a very short amount of time, received a sum of money for unfair dismissal. I am not one for having a fight for a fight's sake, but I cannot abide shabby treatment, and this was shabby.

Being me, I was determined to keep it professional and not personal. As the months and years have gone on, we remain on friendly terms and, of course, Beryl and I continue to live (very happily) on the Wootton Wawen site. Beryl never forgave them.

Even before that was resolved, however, I had found alternative work. My discussion with Allen's was on a Saturday. By Monday morning both myself and Beryl were employed by Morrisons, Stratford-upon-Avon. I rung up the store and a guy called Julian answered the phone. He told me that the manager, Martin, was on a day off.

'Come in tomorrow, Clive, and see Martin. This is like Aldershot Football Club signing Messi,' he said.

Julian had been my produce manager in 1986 in Presto Evesham.

The next day, Martin told us that he would be delighted to have Beryl and I work at Stratford-upon-Avon Morrisons.

I had not been without work since the age of 15, and even at 67 I wasn't going to break the record of a lifetime!

I had worked at the store when it was Safeway. Simon Whitmore opened the store in around 1996 and I supported him for one week. An incident I remember from this time was when a gentlemen brought in a suit that he needed to clean for a wedding. Unfortunately, a girl left the arm sticking out of the drier door and the arm was ripped off. Simon asked me my opinion of what he should do. I said, 'You have two options. One, you could use it and go to a fancy dress as Wurzel Gummidge; two, you could simply give me the money for the new suit.'

Today, aged 81, I continue at Morrisons. Beryl resigned only in 2023, at age 73.

I just love retail! I start at 4.45 a.m. and finish at 12 p.m. or 1 p.m.. I would hate to start at 9 a.m., as it would feel like I had wasted so much of the day. This way, I have the afternoons off and of an evening I aim to be in bed by 9 p.m.

Being on the shop floor, rather than SGM, means my days are very different from how they were in Safeway Evesham. I enjoy scanning and organising stock, using the ever-more automated methods of the 2020s. There is still plenty of stress and pressure, but there are four colleagues who make the stress manageable: Neil, Steve, Brenda and her daughter Helen.

The hardest thing, perhaps, is how I hold back – or try to – from telling management how I would run the store and perhaps do things differently to maximise sales. These days, there isn't the natural skill in the job that there used to be. As a manager, I did things that I knew were in the interest of customers and sales. Today, store managers have to follow head office instructions, down to the tiniest of details, whether they are great or less great decisions.

I talk about it all with Beryl, of course, and we chuckle about the opportunities for displaying promotions that the store seems to regularly miss! It takes me back more than 50 years to when we worked alongside each other at Pearks West Bromwich. Happy days.

In Steve s Garden in Chard , Early days , looks a bit different now.

Children of Harvington School , Seed Collection, for the Schools in Gambia , when at Presto Evesham .

Adam (Carls son) Steve n Carl.

Haydn, Colleague for many years still in touch even now.

15: STILL SO MUCH AHEAD

I may be 81, but retirement is not on the horizon. I continue to love the buzz that is retail. I continue to be mentally agile and physically fit enough to put in a very full early shift at Morrisons then still have the energy and enthusiasm for a session of crown green bowling at Wootton. I play several times a week during the spring and summer season with my good friend George Donaldson. In August 2023, the team won the cup and against the favourites in the division, too. As ever, when there was pressure I upped my performance to score a 21 to 13 win.

Certainly, I don't see myself slowing down any time soon. More of what I do now would be very nice indeed.

It's taken nearly two years from the first words to this final chapter. It had been on my mind for decades to compile my life story, but it was two years ago that, from my Gambian home, I first put pen to paper. It's been wonderful to review the amazing life and times I have enjoyed. to re-examine favourite moments and memories, and to reflect on the challenges. Now, finally, I need to say a few thank yous and sum up my views.

As my family and I have travelled through life, there have been so many lovely memories, but, of course, I have also had my share of heartache along the way. Overall, however, I consider myself highly fortunate. I think being grateful for all the memories we have been able to make is highly important in life.

Like many dads, I have sacrificed a few things along the way to make sure my kids have not gone without. This was especially true when they were very small and we lived in a flat above a shop. I totally understand that you get 'nothing for nothing' in this world (and I hope I have passed that message on down the generations). It feels important to add directly to my boys that it has been a pleasure to work hard all of my life to provide for you. In this life, you have to work hard and also to stand up for what you believe in and for those whom you love. I am remembering now how even from an early age Carl and Steve looked out for each other.

Of my two boys, Steve is most like me in that if he sees an issue, he will work out a plan and get it sorted. At work, he also takes my approach: let me focus on what's gone wrong; what's going well will take care of itself.

Carl is more reflective and sensitive, except when it comes to sport. Then he is determined to win! When he was 17, he went tenpin bowling. He made the local paper, the *Redditch Advertiser*, when he scored 13 strikes on a trot to total the maximum of 360. Carl has always had a great eye for things and was similarly strong at darts, football, cricket and pool.

Talking of pool, this reminds me of a time I bet few of our pool team will ever forget. James Ford still often talks about the night we were playing in Dumbleton; in fact, he *insists* on bringing it up, for reasons that will become clear...

It was a cold night and I had to stand next to the open fire to keep warm. The guy I was playing against had his arm in a sling because he had broken it. I don't remember his name. He was still able to cue but, naturally perhaps, I expected to defeat him. He was left with one black to pot. I had one stripe still on the table, but he was snookered. He hit the white, it bounced off two cushions and hit the black, which then hit a cushion and ended up in the pocket. To be defeated by a guy with a broken arm in a sling – to say I was pissed off is an understatement!

Carl and Steve have both been brilliant dads. I hold the hope that in all the many, many hours we spent together as they were growing up, I was able to be a role model on how taking an interest and really listening to what your children have to say is most important in life. I love my boys as my sons, and I like them very much for the men that they have become.

I would also like to thank JC for all his hard work in looking after us on the journey that we are taking. I'm sure I will one day join the rest of my family who have taken the same pathway and now passed on. When I am with them once more, I will reminisce about our years of plenty.

Neither of my brothers is still living. I am sure that I will see them again, as well as Mom and Dad. It is my family that have made my life so memorable. As well as my parents and brothers, I am thinking now about Uncle Arthur, who taught me so much about the world around me. Thank you, Arthur! I hope I have done you proud.

Also, in thanking people who have made my life what it has been, I certainly cannot forget Snick, my best friend ever, a true mate for 80 years.

Finally in this life story, I want to say a message to my lovely wife of nearly 55 years. Without you, Beryl, this book could not have been written. I love you very much and cannot thank you enough for all you have done (and continue to do) in looking after me and our family: Carl, Steven, Carl's children, Adam and Lauren, and Steve's daughter, Cynthia.

More generally, to anyone who reads my story, remember that whatever problems you may face in life, there is always hope.

Barvie and Cynthia, in the Gambia Cynthia in her Sebec uniform

S O S, School, that we sent school items for the children, again the Gambia , Beryl and Tijan. with the kids.

Steve, Barvie n Cynthia, Lynmouth , Slave Trader, ?

Muss , Steves first cat, in the Gambia, rip Muss, miss you. shes playing with Marriam, Steves other cat, rip Marriam

Adam (Carls son) West Midland Safari Park, very excited about something.

Our home now, at Wootton Wawen. Retirement park,, "Brookside"., lovely spot by the River ,

GLOSSARY: NICKNAMES AND THEIR ORIGINS

Real name: Snick's mum
Nickname: Dirty Legs
Reason for nickname: She went to the doctor with a bad foot. She had washed only the bad foot, but the doctor told her to take her other shoe and sock off, and her foot was black. 'Go back, wash that one and come back,' she was told!

Real Name: The postman
Nickname: Tick-Tock
Reason for nickname: He was at each postbox like clockwork. We would wind him up by shouting 'tick-tock' when we saw him and swinging our arms like pendulums. Once, he was so annoyed he stuffed Snick into the box on the front of his post office bike and rode off. We stopped doing it after that.

Real Name: Mr Elliot, the farmer
Nickname: Square Arse
Reason for nickname: Snick and I would see him as he bent down to use a 'spud' – a chisel-bladed weeding tool. He

would stand on this spud and from behind he looked the shape of his nickname.

Real Name: Fred, my dad's brother
Nickname: Tetnal
Reason for nickname: It's a variety of pear and Fred used to do all his courting under that tree!

Real name: Larry, my brother
Nickname: Lazza and Big 'Un
Reason for nickname: On account of him being the eldest!

Real name: Irwin, my brother
Nickname: He liked to be called John or Middle 'Un
Reason for nickname: Irwin didn't like his birth name, and Middle 'Un came from him being the middle brother.

Real name: Ben, my dad
Nickname: Wicket
Reason for nickname: Dad was umpire at the local cricket club.

Real Name: Tom Smith, Mom's partner
Nickname: Tiger
Reason for nickname: Tom was given this nickname after he hit a man, who was part of the Windrush generation, over the head with a shovel during an altercation over a blast furnace at the factory where he worked.

Real Name: Brian
Nickname: Mucka Bri
Reason for nickname: He was just a mucka of Larry.

Finally, and never forgotten:

- Sal, Beryl's mum, and George, Beryl's dad
- Shirley, Beryl's sister
- Jenny, Shirley's daughter
- Pauline, Beryl's sister
- Terry, Pauline's husband
- Ben, my dad
- Gladys, my mum
- Larry, my brother
- Irwin, my brother
- Arthur, my uncle

More Flood damage at Weir Meadow, Evesham. Muka Bry, with one of the residents.

Cynthia, with her Nan n Grandad , Gambia , "When you taking me to the uk ?)

Steves house in the Gambia

Beryl , looking very tanned ,. at the Clay Oven,, best Indian Eating House in the Gambia , without a doubt.

Beryl on a visit to Maliks Mom, in Ebo town the Gambia ,, as she does every year,

StoryTerrace

Printed in Great Britain
by Amazon